WORLD COOKERY

Marguerite Patten began her career as a demonstrator with a fuel company and, during the war, worked as a senior demonstrator with the Ministry of Food, showing women how to keep their families fit on the available rations. From 1943–50 she was responsible for the Food Advice and Home Service Advice Bureau at Harrods. During this time, she was invited to broadcast on early morning household and cooking programmes and began regular BBC TV cookery programmes in 1947. When, in 1956, BBC TV started their Cookery Club, Marguerite Patten became President, and for five years viewers sent in recipes which she tested on television. She demonstrates and gives lectures throughout Britain and has also worked on Australian television. She now writes regularly for *Woman's Own* and has had over sixty cookery books published.

Marguerite Patten lives in Brighton with her husband and has one daughter.

Also available in Pan Books

LEARNING TO COOK
Marguerite Patten

DEEP-FREEZE COOKERY
Marika Hanbury Tenison

THE CORDON BLEU BOOK OF JAMS, PRESERVES AND PICKLES
Rosemary Hume and Muriel Downes

ALL ABOUT COOKERY
Mrs Beeton

HERBS FOR HEALTH AND COOKERY
Claire Loewenfeld and Philippa Back

MISS READ'S COUNTRY COOKING

Six ROBERT CARRIER PARTY BOOKS

World Cookery

Marguerite Patten

Illustrated by Rosemary Aldridge

A PAN ORIGINAL
PAN BOOKS LTD : LONDON

First published 1972 by Pan Books Ltd,
33 Tothill Street, London, SW1.

ISBN 0 330 02952 5

© The Hamlyn Publishing Group Ltd, 1972

Made and printed in Great Britain by
Cox & Wyman Ltd, London, Reading and Fakenham

Contents

Introduction

Whoever we are, wherever we are, we can't help
but take an interest in other people's food. For
every country, what they eat and how they cook
is of their national heritage — and it is very
exciting to try various dishes when abroad or in
foreign restaurants, and what is more natural
than to want to make those we find particularly
tasty when we return home!

In this book I have collected those recipes
which are most universally popular. None is
difficult or extravagant and most ingredients
are easy to obtain from good grocers, delicatessens
or specialist food shops. Occasionally, I have
substituted ingredients to make the dish easier
to prepare, just as good cooks do with their
native dishes when certain ingredients are
unobtainable because they're out of season or in
short supply for some other reason.

Marguerite Patten

Wines

Most countries with mild climates in the growing
seasons make their own wines. Some make vast
quantities of good wine for everyday drinking,
and also make finer wines which are more
expensive, but which are just right for special
occasions. It is interesting that though there are
only one or two private vineyards in Britain, we
have for centuries been eager buyers and
consumers of the best wines from other countries
all over the world – and it would appear from the
statistics that our consumption of wines increases
quite considerably every year. Many countries
covered in this cookery book produce excellent
wines but I have left it to you to make your
choice of wines because so much depends on your
own taste, how much you want to spend, and
what is available from your local supplier.

Guide to Good Cooking

WEIGHTS AND MEASURES

English weights and measures have been used throughout this book.

The average English teacup holds $\frac{1}{4}$ pint. The average English breakfast cup holds $\frac{1}{2}$ pint. Eight tablespoons liquid measures equal $\frac{1}{4}$ pint. In case it is wished to translate any of the weights and measures into their American or metric counterparts, the following notes and table give a comparison.

LIQUID MEASURE

The most important difference to be noted is that the American (US) pint is 16 fluid ounces, as opposed to the British Imperial pint and Australian and Canadian pints which are 20 fluid ounces. The US $\frac{1}{2}$-pint measuring cup (8 fluid ounces) is equivalent to two-fifths of a British pint. A British $\frac{1}{2}$-pint measuring cup (10 fluid ounces) is equal to $1\frac{1}{4}$ US cups.

METRIC WEIGHTS AND MEASURES

It is difficult to convert to metric measures with absolute accuracy, but 1 oz is equal to approximately 25 grammes, 1 lb is equal to approximately 450 grammes, 2 lb 3 oz to 1 kilogramme. For liquid measure $1\frac{3}{4}$ British pints (35 fluid ounces) equals approximately 1 litre; 1 demilitre is half a litre ($17\frac{1}{2}$ fluid ounces), and 1 decilitre is one-tenth of a litre ($3\frac{1}{2}$ fluid ounces). 1 UK tablespoon equals 18 ml. 1 UK teaspoon equals 6 ml.

SOLID MEASURE

British	American
1 lb butter or other fat	2 cups
1 lb flour	4 cups
1 lb granulated or caster sugar	2 cups
1 lb icing or confectioners' sugar	3 cups
1 lb brown (moist) sugar	2½ cups
1 lb golden syrup or treacle	1 cup
1 lb rice	2 cups
1 lb dried fruit	2 cups (well filled)
1 lb chopped meat (finely packed)	2 cups
1 lb lentils or split peas	2 cups
1 lb coffee (unground)	2¼ cups
1 lb soft breadcrumbs	5 cups
1 oz caster sugar	2 tablespoons
1 oz demerara sugar	2 tablespoons
1 oz granulated sugar	2 tablespoons
1 oz icing sugar	4 tablespoons
1 oz soft brown sugar	3 tablespoons

All US standard measuring tablespoons

BRITISH TABLESPOON (LEVEL) AND OUNCE EQUIVALENTS

NOTE: these measurements are approximate, and therefore must not be used for larger quantities than 2 oz. The tablespoon measures are level, as are all spoon measures in this book.

Commodity	Tablespoons	Ounces
Sugars		
caster sugar	2	1 oz
demerara sugar	2	1 oz
granulated sugar	2	1 oz
icing sugar	4	1 oz
soft brown sugar	3	1 oz
Syrups and Jams		
golden syrup	1	1 oz
honey	1	1 oz
treacle	1	¾ oz
jam	1	1 oz

Commodity	Tablespoons	Ounces
Nuts		
ground almonds	3	1 oz
18 whole almonds	—	1 oz
chopped hazelnuts	3	1 oz
whole hazelnuts	2	1 oz
whole pistachios	2	1 oz
chopped walnuts	3	1 oz
8 walnut halves	—	1 oz
Crumbs		
dried breadcrumbs	6	1 oz
fresh breadcrumbs	7	1 oz
packet crumbs	4	1 oz
Dried fruit		
currants	2	1 oz
8 glacé cherries	—	1 oz
cut peel	1	1 oz
seedless raisins	2	1 oz
sultanas	2	1 oz
Miscellaneous		
flour	1	$\frac{1}{2}$ oz
arrowroot	2	1 oz
cocoa powder	3	1 oz
desiccated coconut	4	1 oz
ground coffee	4	1 oz
instant coffee	7	1 oz
cornflour	2	1 oz
sugar	1	1 oz
butter	1	$\frac{1}{2}$ oz
jelly	1	1 oz
curry powder	4	1 oz
custard powder	2	1 oz
flour	3	1 oz
rolled oats	4	1 oz
instant potato powder	2	1 oz
rice	2	1 oz
ground rice	3	1 oz
semolina	2	1 oz

OVEN TEMPERATURES

Description	Electric Setting	Gas Mark
very cool	225 degrees F. (110°C.)	$\frac{1}{4}$
	250 degrees F. (130°C.)	$\frac{1}{2}$
cool	275 degrees F. (140°C.)	1
	300 degrees F. (150°C.)	2
very moderate	325 degrees F. (170°C.)	3
moderate	350 degrees F. (180°C.)	4
moderately or	375 degrees F. (190°C.)	5
fairly hot	400 degrees F. (200°C.)	6
hot	425 degrees F. (220°C.)	7
	450 degrees F. (230°C.)	8
very hot	475 degrees F. (240°C.)	9

These temperatures are only an approximate guide as all ovens vary slightly, according to the make.

WORKING OUT METRIC EQUIVALENTS

Oz	gm taking 1 oz = 28·4 gm	Approximation to nearest 5 gm	Error in gm	gm taking 1 oz = 30 gm	Error in gm	gm taking 1 oz = 25 gm	Error in gm
1	28·4	30	+1·6	30	+1·6	25	−3·4
2	56·8	55	−1·8	60	+3·2	50	−6·4
3	85·2	85	−0·2	90	+4·8	75	−10·2
4	113·6	115	+1·4	120	+6·4	100	−13·6
5	142·0	140	−2·0	150	+8·0	125	−17·0
6	170·4	170	−0·4	180	+9·6	150	−20·4
7	198·8	200	+1·4	210	+11·2	175	−23·8
8	227·2	225	−2·2	240	+12·8	200	−27·2
12	340·8	340	−0·8	360	+19·2	300	−40·8
16	454·4	455	+0·6	480	+25·6	400	−54·4

AUSTRIA, GERMANY and SWITZERLAND

Austria

Austria is essentially a gay country with light-hearted music wherever you go. The cafés are a way of life and the rich cream cakes tempt even the most figure-conscious person! You will find several recipes for cakes in this chapter, all of which are easily made.

Because Austria has no coastline the fish are freshwater fish and the Austrian housewife has developed very clever ideas for these (see page 7). Many of the Austrian meat dishes are very similar to those of the bordering country, Hungary, in that they use sour cream and paprika for flavouring.

Germany

Although Germany is a close neighbour to Austria, and in some ways has similar eating habits, German food is usually more substantial and sustaining. German yeast cakes (see page 16) are famous. Various types of sausage including frankfurters are very popular and they are often served with sauerkraut.

Switzerland

Mountainous Switzerland is surrounded by Italy, France, Austria and Germany, each of which has added something to the Swiss cuisine. The Swiss national dish is Cheese Fondue, which should properly be made with Swiss Gruyère cheese (see page 5). It's very popular as an informal party dish as it makes a wonderful centrepiece.

Soups in these countries are of infinite variety, ranging from family vegetable soups to the wine soups (Weinsuppe) of Germany which make a most unusual start to a meal.

Wine Soup   Germany

Weinsuppe

4–6 servings

1 pint white wine	2–3 egg yolks
1 pint water	1 teaspoon sugar
One 2-inch stick cinnamon	Salt and pepper
Lemon rind	

Heat the wine (sparkling Moselle is excellent) and water with the stick of cinnamon and a little lemon rind. Blend the egg yolks with 1 tablespoon water, add to the soup and thicken slowly over a low heat (potato flour is often used as a thickening agent instead of eggs). Stir well and do not allow to boil. Remove cinnamon and lemon rind before serving. Add the sugar, salt and pepper to taste, just before serving.

Bread Soup

Brot Suppe

4 servings

3 slices bread
1½ pints veal stock
Salt and pepper

1–2 egg yolks
Cooked sausage, chopped
Parsley, finely chopped

Crisp the bread in a cool oven, then break into small pieces and put in a pan. Reserve 2 tablespoons of stock, add the rest to the bread with salt and pepper to taste, and simmer for 30 minutes until the bread disintegrates and the soup is smooth. Add egg yolks blended with the reserved stock, and thicken without boiling, stirring all the time. Garnish with cooked sausage and parsley.

Cucumber Purée Soup

Austria

Gurkensuppe

4 servings

2 medium cucumbers,
  chopped
1 onion, chopped
1 stick celery, chopped
¾ pint white stock
1 oz butter

1 oz flour
½ pint milk
Salt and pepper
Little lemon juice or
  vinegar (optional)
Parsley, finely chopped

Mix the cucumber, onion and celery together. Put into a pan with the stock and simmer until tender. Rub through a sieve. Make a white sauce with the butter, flour and milk. Add the vegetable purée, reheat and season well. Add a little lemon juice or vinegar, if wished, but do not let it boil again. Serve garnished with chopped parsley.

Golden Dumplings in Beef Consommé

Germany

4–6 servings

1 oz butter, melted
4 oz self-raising flour, sieved
Salt and pepper

1 small egg plus 1 yolk
Milk to mix
1½ pints beef consommé
Parsley, finely chopped

Add melted butter to flour with a pinch of salt and pepper. Add the eggs and, if necessary, add a few drops of milk to make the mixture into a pliable dough. Roll into tiny balls the size of an acorn and cook for 10–15 minutes in the beef consommé. Garnish with parsley.

Cheese Fondue

Switzerland

8 servings

Unsalted butter
1 lb Gruyère or Emmenthal cheese, grated
Salt and pepper to taste
½ pint dry white wine

1 teaspoon cornflour (optional)
1 tablespoon brandy or Curaçao (optional)
Bite-size squares of toast or bread

5

It is possible to buy special fondue pans and heaters to ensure the cheese mixture is kept at the right temperature.

Grease the bottom and sides of an ovenproof dish or fondue pan with a little butter. Add the cheese, seasoning and the wine. Some people blend 1 teaspoon cornflour with a little of the wine and add to the mixture to prevent the mixture curdling. Keep warm over a gentle heat and stir from time to time. If liked, a little brandy or Curaçao can be added. Do not let the mixture boil quickly or the cheese becomes tough. Serve Cheese Fondue with squares of toast or bread.

Spear the squares with a fork, dip them in the cheese mixture, and eat them while hot.

Bismarck Herrings   Germany

Bismarckheringe

4–6 servings

6 herrings
1–1½ pint vinegar
Salt

Cayenne pepper
2 onions, thinly sliced

Scale and clean herrings, but leave on the heads. Put into a dish, cover with the vinegar and leave for 24 hours. Lift from vinegar, remove heads and backbone. Cut each herring into 2 fillets. Arrange in dish, sprinkle generously with salt and pepper and thinly sliced onions. Leave for at least 24 hours before using. The vinegar can be strained, boiled well and kept for use again with fish.

Fish with Capers

Austria

4 servings

4 onions, sliced
2 oz butter
1½ lb carp or white fish
Salt and pepper
¼ pint cultured sour cream

Rind of 1 lemon, finely
    grated plus juice of ½
    lemon
2–3 teaspoons chopped
    parsley
1–2 tablespoons capers

If cultured sour cream is not available, use fresh cream and one extra tablespoon lemon juice.

Fry the onions in butter until soft. Add the fish cut into neat pieces together with seasoning, and cook for about 5 minutes. Stir in sour cream and lemon rind and juice, parsley and capers. Continue cooking for 10 minutes. Serve hot.

Fish in Cream Sauce

Austria

Fisch mit Rahm

4–6 servings

1½ lb white fish or carp
Salt and pepper
Juice ½ lemon
¼ pint cultured sour cream

4 tablespoons grated
    Parmesan cheese
1½ oz butter
Parsley sprigs

If cultured sour cream is not available, use fresh cream and one extra tablespoon lemon juice.

7

Skin the fish and place in a baking dish. Season with salt and pepper, add lemon juice. Pour the cream over the fish. Sprinkle with the Parmesan cheese. Dot with the butter. Bake in a moderately hot oven for about 20 minutes, basting occasionally with the cream. Garnish with parsley.

Chicken with Paprika Sauce   Austria

Paprikahuhn

4 servings

8 small rashers bacon
1 oz butter
4 chicken pieces
Hot water
Salt

1 tablespoon paprika
½ pint cultured sour cream
4–6 oz rice, boiled in
   plenty of hot water

If cultured sour cream is not available, use fresh cream with one extra tablespoon lemon juice.

Fry the rashers in a little butter in a large frying-pan, taking care not to overcook them. Remove from the pan and keep warm in a very cool oven. Fry the chicken pieces in the bacon fat until they are golden. Add a little hot water and simmer until they are quite tender, seasoning with salt and paprika. Add the cream gradually, stirring until the sauce thickens. Put boiled rice in the centre of a serving dish and cover with the bacon rashers. Arrange the chicken and sauce round the dish .

Veal or pork chops can be used as an alternative to chicken in this recipe.

Fillets of Veal

Austria

Wiener Schnitzel

4–6 servings

1½ lb veal fillet
Salt and pepper
3 tablespoons flour
1 egg

1 tablespoon water
Crisped breadcrumbs
2–3 oz fat or butter
1 lemon, sliced

Cut the fillet into 4–6 neat pieces and beat until very thin, or get your butcher to prepare them for you.

Add salt and pepper to the flour and mix well. Mix the egg and water together. Coat each fillet in the seasoned flour. Then dip into the beaten egg and water. Coat with the breadcrumbs. Press these firmly on to the veal, shaking off any surplus. Fry in hot fat or butter until golden brown on either side. Reduce heat and cook gently until tender. Serve garnished with lemon slices.

Pork Chops with Frankfurters and Sauerkraut

Germany

Schwein Ekoteletts mit Sauerkraut

4 servings

4 pork chops
Salt and pepper
3 oz butter
8 oz frankfurters
Boiling water

1 green pepper, sliced
  (optional)
2 eating apples, cored and
  sliced
1 lb bought sauerkraut
Parsley

Season the pork chops with salt and pepper, brush with I oz melted butter and grill until golden and tender. Keep warm. Gently simmer frankfurters in boiling water for 5–6 minutes until tender. Score and drain. Melt the rest of the butter and fry green pepper and apples until cooked. Meanwhile, heat sauerkraut and season. Turn on to a dish. Arrange pork chops and frankfurters on the bed of sauerkraut and garnish with green pepper, apples and parsley.

Apple Strudel   Austria

Apfel Strudel

8–10 servings

Strudel dough:
8 oz plain flour
Pinch salt
I egg yolk
I tablespoon melted butter
  or oil
$\frac{1}{4}$ pint warm water

For the filling:
2 oz breadcrumbs
4 oz melted butter
$1\frac{1}{2}$ lb cooking apples,
  peeled, cored and sliced
2 oz currants
2 oz stoned raisins
2 oz caster sugar
1–2 teaspoons powdered
  cinnamon
Grated rind $\frac{1}{2}$ lemon

Sieve the flour and salt together, stir in the egg yolk, the table-spoon of melted butter or oil and sufficient water to make a soft dough. Knead on a warm floured board. When smooth, cover with a warm cloth and bowl. Stand for approximately 15 minutes.

Fry the crumbs in half the melted butter. Carefully mix with the remaining ingredients. Cover table with a clean cloth. Sprinkle with flour, place dough in the middle, roll out as thinly as possible with floured rolling pin. Gently pull dough outwards from the middle, using mainly the balls of the thumbs. It should be pulled out thin enough to read through, but this takes practice. Spread apple mixture over the dough to within $\frac{1}{2}$ inch of the edges. Roll up like a Swiss roll, lift on to a baking sheet, curve into horseshoe if necessary. Brush with some of the remaining melted butter and bake in centre of a hot oven for 20 minutes. Reduce to moderate, and continue baking for 30 minutes. Brush with melted butter two or three times during baking. Serve sliced, hot or cold, with whipped cream.

Variations

Chocolate Apple Strudel. Add 2 oz drinking chocolate to the ingredients for the filling.

Plum Strudel. Use plums and sultanas in place of apples and raisins.

Cheese Cake   Switzerland

Gâteau au Fromage

10–12 servings

Biscuit Crust:
6 oz plain flour
4 oz butter
1 oz sugar
1 egg yolk

Filling:
3 oz butter
3 oz sugar
Grated rind and juice of 1
    lemon
12 oz cream cheese
3 eggs

Make a rich biscuit crust pastry with the flour, 4 oz butter, 1 oz sugar and 1 egg yolk. Line a 9-inch tin with the pastry. Whip the egg whites until stiff.

Cream together the remaining butter, sugar, grated lemon

rind, then add the 3 egg yolks, lemon juice, cream cheese and the egg whites. Put into the pastry case and bake in the centre of a slow to very moderate oven for 1 hour until set. Cool in the oven with heat turned off.

Variation
Add 1 oz cornflour to egg yolk mixture, plus 2 oz dried fruit and 1–2 oz chopped candied peel.

Chocolate Cream   Austria

Schokoladen Koch

2–3 servings

2 oz plain chocolate	2 eggs, separated
2 tablespoons water	Whipped cream
1 tablespoon concentrated coffee	Strawberries or nuts

Melt the chocolate in a saucepan over a low heat with the water and coffee. Beat the yolks and stir into the chocolate. Whip the whites until stiff and fold into the chocolate mixture. When set, top with whipped cream and strawberries or nuts.

Spiced Tart   Austria

Linzertorte

6–8 servings

6 oz margarine or butter
2 oz caster sugar
2 oz ground almonds,
   hazelnuts or walnuts
Grated rind of 1 lemon
1 egg
8 oz plain flour sieved
   with ½ teaspoon cinnamon

1 lb fresh raspberries,
   cooked and sweetened or
   1 large can raspberries
   (drained) or 1 lb
   raspberry jam
2 tablespoons redcurrant
   jelly
Icing sugar

Cream the fat and sugar, add the nuts, lemon rind, egg and 2 tablespoons flour and cinnamon mixture; and mix well. Add the remaining flour and stir together to form a soft dough. Turn on to a lightly floured board and knead lightly with the fingertips to a smooth dough. Roll out two-thirds of the dough and line an 8-inch fluted flan ring placed on a baking sheet. Chill for 30 minutes. Roll out remaining pastry and cut into strips ¼ inch wide and 8½ inches long. Fill the flan case with the raspberries and arrange the pastry strips in a lattice across the top of the flan. Bake in the centre of a moderately hot oven for 30–35 minutes. Melt the redcurrant jelly and brush over the fruit to glaze. Dust lightly with icing sugar.

Light Plain Cake   Austria
Gugelhupf

8–10 servings

4½ oz butter, softened   4 eggs
4½ oz caster sugar   4½ oz plain flour
Grated rind 1 lemon

Cream softened butter, sugar and finely grated rind of lemon until very light and fluffy. Gradually beat in egg yolks. Stir sieved flour into egg yolk mixture. Whisk egg whites until stiff and fold evenly into the mixture. Fill a greased and floured fluted tin or gugelhupf mould (obtainable from ironmongers specializing in continental kitchen utensils) three-quarters full. Bake in the centre of a moderate oven for about 30–40 minutes.

Hazelnut Gâteau   Austria
Nusstorte

6–8 servings

3 oz flour   ¼ pint cream
Pinch salt   2 tablespoons clear honey
3 eggs   Small can sliced peaches or
4½ oz caster sugar   fresh peaches (optional)
1 tablespoon coffee essence   Icing sugar
2 oz browned ground or   A few whole hazelnuts
   chopped hazelnuts

Grease and flour two 8-inch sandwich tins.

Sieve the flour and salt. Whisk the eggs, sugar and coffee essence in a basin over a bowl of hot water, until beginning to thicken. Remove from the heat and whisk until cold. Fold in the sieved flour and nuts. Divide mixture between the sandwich tins and bake for about 25 minutes in a moderate oven until firm.

Whip the cream and blend it with the honey. Spread most of this on one cake, then top with peaches and place the other cake on top. Dredge with icing sugar. Decorate with the remaining cream and whole hazelnuts.

Cherry Gâteau   Austria

Kirschtorte

8–10 servings

6 oz butter or margarine
6 oz caster sugar
3 eggs
6 oz flour (with plain flour use 1½ level teaspoon baking powder)
Little warm water
2 teaspoons cocoa
3 teaspoons boiling water

4 oz hazelnuts
2 oz glacé, canned, or fresh ripe cherries
Cream or butter cream (see following recipe)
2 oz toasted flaked almonds
Marzipan cherries if available

Grease and line three 7-inch sandwich tins.

Cream the fat and sugar until light and fluffy. Beat in the eggs. Fold in the sieved flour, adding sufficient warm water to make a soft dropping consistency. Divide two-thirds of the mixture between two of the sandwich tins. Blend the cocoa with the boiling water and stir into remaining sponge mixture. Spread this evenly in a third tin. Bake for about 20–25 minutes above the centre of a moderate oven. Chop the hazelnuts, reserving 12 whole nuts for decoration. Stone the cherries if necessary and chop into small pieces. Add the chopped nuts and cherries to the butter cream.

Sandwich the three cakes together with some of the butter cream, placing the chocolate layer in the centre. Spread more butter cream evenly round the sides of the gâteau, dip into the almonds. Spread the remaining butter cream on top. Decorate with the whole hazelnuts. If liked, top with marzipan cherries.

Butter Cream

6 oz unsalted butter
9 oz icing sugar, sieved

Few drops vanilla essence
Very little milk

Cream the butter and sugar until very soft and white. Gradually beat in the vanilla essence and enough milk to give a soft dropping consistency. Use as required.

Yeast Cakes   Germany

Kurlich

8–10 servings

1 teaspoon sugar
8 tablespoons milk and water mixed
1 level tablespoon dried yeast or 1 oz fresh yeast
1 lb plain flour
1 teaspoon salt
4 oz sugar
2 oz currants

2 oz blanched almonds, chopped
½ teaspoon vanilla essence
3 tablespoons oil or melted butter
2 eggs
Glacé icing
Hundreds and thousands

16

Dissolve the teaspoon sugar in warm milk and water, sprinkle the dried yeast on top, or blend the fresh yeast with sugar and liquid. Leave until frothy, approximately 10 minutes.

Mix together the flour and salt, add the sugar, currants and almonds. Add the yeast liquid, vanilla essence, oil or butter and eggs. Mix well together until dough leaves the sides of the bowl clean. Turn out on to lightly floured board, knead well for 5 minutes. Prove in a warm place for about 2 hours until dough practically doubles in size. Turn on to lightly floured board and knead. Shape pieces of dough to half-fill well-greased tins. Cover each tin with polythene or a clean cloth. Leave the dough to prove for 40–60 minutes, or until it springs back when lightly pressed with a floured finger. Bake in centre of a moderately hot oven for about 40 minutes. When cold, trail the glacé icing over the top and edges of the cake and sprinkle with hundreds and thousands.

Belgium and Holland

Belgium

The food in Belgium is an intriguing mixture of French and Flemish with certain outstanding recipes of their own. As they have a small coast line, fish dishes are plentiful and good in Belgium.

Chicory is among the most famous of Belgian vegetables; it is delicious served raw or cooked and it is also exported.

Meat in Belgium is good, beef and veal being the most popular, and Carbonnade of beef is a world-famous dish.

Holland

Holland is such a near neighbour to France and Belgium, it is amazing that the food here is really so different. Much of it is highly spiced, as spices have been introduced from the Dutch colonies in the East.

Soups are filling and sustaining; salt fish is used extensively, and the meat dishes are not unlike those of Germany. Fairly substantial vegetables such as peas and potatoes are particularly popular in Holland.

Dutch sweets are simple; pancakes, fritters and dumplings are served with well-spiced sauces.

Fish, in particular eel, is used in both countries as an hors d'oeuvre. Smoked eel makes a delicious hors d'oeuvre. Salt herrings and bloaters are extremely popular in Holland.

In Belgium there is an excellent fish soup not unlike Bouillabaisse (see page 69) called Le Waterzoie de Poissons: prawns are cooked in a vegetable-flavoured fish stock with or without wine and served hot in the liquid.

Eel Soup   Holland

Aasoep

6 servings

8 oz eel	2 oz butter
3 pints cold salted water	2 oz flour
1 onion, sliced	12 capers
Parsley sprigs and chopped parsley	

Put the eel pieces into the water, bring to the boil, cover pan, and simmer for about 1 hour. Add the onion and parsley sprigs. Heat the butter in another pan, blend with the flour, then strain the eel stock over this. Bring to the boil and cook until thickened, add a few capers and chopped parsley together with the pieces of eel.

Eel in Green Sauce   Belgium

6–8 servings

2–2½ lb young eels
4 oz butter
Salt and pepper
2 teaspoons each of chopped
  chervil, mint, parsley,
  sage and sorrel (or more
  if liked)

½ pint dry white wine
¾ pint water
3 egg yolks
Juice of 1 lemon

Skin the eels – remove heads and cut into 1½ to 2-inch lengths.
Heat 2 oz butter, add eels, seasoning, and herbs. Toss eels in this
mixture for about 10 minutes. Cover with wine, add ½ pint water.
Simmer for 15 minutes. Blend the egg yolks with remaining
water. Stir into the eel mixture with the lemon juice and remaining butter. Heat gently, spoon into dishes. Serve cold.

Fishcakes   Holland

2–3 servings

8 oz cooked white fish,
  chopped
4 oz mashed potatoes
2 oz breadcrumbs
Salt and pepper

1 egg, beaten
Little milk
Flour
Oil for frying

Blend the fish with the potatoes and breadcrumbs. Season to
taste. Bind with the egg and a little milk. Coat with flour and fry
in hot fat until crisp.

Hussar's Salad Holland

Huzarensia

4 servings

8 oz stewing steak
Salt and pepper
8–10 boiled potatoes,
  chopped
2 cooked beetroots, diced
1 cooking apple, peeled,
  cored and shredded

Silver onions to taste
Gherkins to taste
French mustard
Mayonnaise
Salad in season

Stew the steak in water with a pinch of salt until tender, then cut into small pieces. Mix with the potatoes, beetroot and apple. Add silver onions, gherkins, salt and pepper, mustard and mayonnaise to taste.

Put the mixture on to a flat dish and garnish with a selection of salad in season and more mayonnaise.

Cooked Chicory Belgium

Chicory is called *endive* in some countries and *witloof* in Belgium!

Simmer in salted water to which a tablespoon of vinegar or lemon juice has been added. Cook for about 15 minutes. Allow at least one head of chicory per person.

Fried Chicory   Belgium

4 servings

4 heads chicory
Oil
1 tablespoon lemon juice

Salt and pepper
Batter (see page 34)

Cook chicory (as on page 23) and drain well. Marinade in 2 tablespoons oil, lemon juice and seasoning, then coat in batter and fry
in oil until golden.

Chicory with Browned Butter   Belgium

4 servings

4 heads chicory
2 oz butter

Cook chicory as above, drain and dry well. Brown the butter by
heating but do not allow to burn. Pour the hot butter over the
chicory and serve immediately.

Rabbit with Prunes   Belgium

Lapin aux pruneaux

4 servings

1 rabbit, jointed	2 oz butter
¾ pint red wine	1½ oz flour
2½ tablespoons vinegar	Salt and pepper
2 bay leaves	1 tablespoon gooseberry
Few peppercorns	or plum jam or
12 oz prunes	redcurrant jelly

Soak the rabbit overnight in the wine, vinegar, bay leaves, and a few peppercorns. In a separate container soak the prunes in cold water.

Next day, remove the rabbit joints from the liquid; dry and cook in butter for a few minutes. Remove rabbit. Blend the flour with the hot butter and cook for several minutes. Add strained wine liquid, bring slowly to the boil, stirring, cook until a smooth sauce. Return the rabbit joints to the pan, add salt and pepper and well-drained prunes. Simmer gently for about 1½ hours until quite tender.

Stir in the jam or jelly just before serving.

Stewed Game   Holland

4–6 servings

Rabbit and hare are also popular in Holland.

Salt and pepper	2 pints stock
1 hare or rabbit, skinned	Pinch grated nutmeg
and jointed	Pinch cinnamon powder
2 oz fat	Vinegar or lemon juice to
1½ oz flour	taste

Salt and pepper the joints and toss in hot fat for a few minutes, add the flour and cook for several minutes. Stir in the stock. Bring to the boil, add the nutmeg, cinnamon, and a little vinegar or lemon juice to taste. Simmer until tender, about 1–1½ hours for young rabbit, about 2½–3 hours for hare.

Stewed Beef   Belgium

Carbonnades de boeuf à la flamande

4–6 servings

4 large onions, thinly sliced	½ pint beer
2 oz dripping or fat	½ pint stock*
1 oz flour	1 teaspoon mustard
Salt and pepper	2 teaspoons sugar
1¼–1½ lb stewing beef, cut in strips	Bouquet garni
2 oz lean bacon	

*If cooking in a casserole, use only ¼ pint stock.

Fry the onions in the hot fat until golden brown. Mix the flour with salt and pepper to taste. Coat the meat in the seasoned flour and fry for several minutes. Add the rest of the ingredients, bring to the boil, stir well, and cook until a smooth sauce is obtained. Either transfer to a covered casserole and cook for about 2 hours in a very moderate oven or lower the ring heat, cover the pan tightly and cook gently for about the same time.

Fried Dumplings   Holland

Oliebollen

4–6 servings

½ oz yeast
1 teaspoon sugar
¼ pint milk
8 oz plain flour
Pinch of salt
1–2 oz sugar
5 oz dried fruit
1 oz candied peel, chopped
Grated rind and juice of
  1 lemon

1 cooking apple, diced
Fat for deep frying
Extra sugar

For the spiced sauce:
1 oz flour or ½ oz cornflour
½ pint milk
1–2 oz brown sugar
Cinnamon to flavour

Cream the yeast with the sugar, milk and a sprinkling of flour.
Allow to stand until mixture bubbles. Add the remaining flour,
salt, the 1–2 oz sugar, dried fruit, candied peel, lemon rind
and the diced apple. Blend well, then add a little lemon juice and
enough milk to give a sticky consistency. Cover and leave in a
warm place for about 1 hour to prove. Heat a pan of deep fat and
drop small balls of the mixture in this and cook until golden
brown. Dust with extra sugar.

Serve with this spiced sauce. Blend the flour or cornflour with
½ pint milk in a pan, add the brown sugar, stir and cook until
thickened. Flavour with plenty of powdered cinnamon, or infuse
a stick of cinnamon in the milk before using.

Yeast Fritters

Holland

Poffertjes

4–6 servings

½ oz fresh yeast	Pinch salt
1 teaspoon sugar	1 teaspoon golden syrup
½ pint tepid milk	1 egg (optional)
9 oz flour	1 oz melted butter

Blend the yeast with the sugar. Add the milk and 1 oz flour. Allow this to bubble, then work in the remaining flour, pinch salt, golden syrup, the egg, if liked, and the melted butter. Half-fill well-greased patty tins with the batter. Allow to prove until doubled in size, then bake for approximately 10 minutes near the top of a hot oven.

Serve immediately topped with jam or sugar, or with the spiced sauce from the Fried Dumplings (see page 27).

Chocolate Cake

Belgium

Gâteau au Chocolat

8–10 servings

2 eggs	3 oz chopped nuts
2 oz caster sugar	2 oz glacé cherries, chopped
4 oz melted butter	½ tablespoon Cognac
8 oz plain chocolate	Few drops vanilla essence
8 oz semi-sweet broken biscuits	

Whisk the eggs and sugar in a basin over hot water until thick. Whisk in cooled melted butter slowly and carefully. Then add the melted chocolate, biscuits, 2 oz chopped nuts, 1 oz chopped glacé cherries, Cognac, and vanilla essence.

Put in a 7- to 8-inch tin with a loose base, top with remaining nuts and cherries.

Allow to set, then cut into neat pieces with a sharp knife.

Great Britain

(England, Ireland, Scotland and Wales)

Great Britain

British food is bland compared to food in many of the other countries mentioned in this book. At its best it is hard to beat because you can taste the food itself, rather than spices and herbs. Britain is renowned for its Fish and Chips (see page 34), Roast Beef and Yorkshire Pudding (see page 35) and Christmas Pudding (see page 37). In fact Britain has a wealth of traditional puddings and cakes and pastries.

Scotch Broth

4–6 servings

1 oz pearl barley
8 oz stewing beef or lamb
2 pints water
3 oz leeks or onions, sliced
8 oz carrots, diced

8 oz swedes, diced
Salt and pepper
2 oz cabbage, chopped
1 tablespoon chopped
  parsley

Blanch barley – put it into cold water, bring to the boil, pour away the water. Put barley, meat and 2 pints water into a pan, bring to the boil, skim. Simmer gently for 1 hour. Either dice meat, or remove from soup to use for a separate dish. Add all prepared vegetables (except cabbage) and the seasoning. Simmer for 1½ hours. Add the cabbage, cook for 15 minutes. Skim off unwanted fat, pour broth into a hot tureen or soup bowls. Garnish with parsley.

Herrings in Oatmeal

Scotland

4 servings

4 large or 8 small herrings
2 oz medium oatmeal

Salt and pepper
Fat for frying

Wash and dry herrings, clean and remove the heads. Mix oatmeal with salt and pepper to taste. Coat fish in the oatmeal and fry in fat until crisp and golden brown.

   This is excellent served with mustard sauce (white sauce seasoned well with mustard) or the recipe on page 133.

33

Kedgeree   Scotland, England

4 servings

1 oz butter
3 oz cooked rice
8–12 oz cooked smoked
   haddock, flaked

1 egg
Milk or cream
Parsley
1 hard-boiled egg, chopped

Heat the butter in a saucepan. Add the rice, fish, raw egg and just a very little milk or cream, then heat together gently, stirring. When ready, pile on to a dish and garnish with parsley and chopped hard-boiled egg.

Although accepted as a British dish, this is based on an Indian dish very similar in appearance, but in which lentils are used in place of haddock (see page 162).

Fried Fish and Chips   England

4 servings

4 portions of white fish

Wash and dry fish, then coat in one of the following:

(a) *Seasoned flour.*
(b) *Flour, then dip in beaten egg and coat with crisp breadcrumbs.*
(c) *Flour, then dip in batter made from 4 oz flour, pinch salt, 1 egg, generous $\frac{1}{4}$ pint milk and water (use a little more for a thin coating) plus 2 teaspoons oil if wished for a crisper coating.*

Fry in deep fat for coating (b) or (c), or shallow fat for either (a) or (b) until fish is crisp and golden brown, then drain on absorbent paper.

   For perfect chipped potatoes, peel and cut potato fingers

neatly, then dry. Fry once in hot fat until tender but not brown, then reheat fat and fry a second time for 1–2 minutes only until really crisp and brown. Drain.

Serve with vinegar and salt and pepper or with Tartare Sauce (mayonnaise which has added chopped capers and chopped gherkins, see page 76), chopped parsley or tomato ketchup.

Roast Beef and Yorkshire Pudding   England

Beef – particularly Scotch beef – is excellent, and most suitable for roasting. The best cuts to choose are sirloin or rib.

The meat should be roasted in a hot oven with a little fat. For rare beef – really red inside – allow 15 minutes per pound, and 15 minutes over; for medium, 20 minutes per pound, and 20 minutes over; for well done (not often cooked as much as this), 25 minutes per pound, and 25 minutes over.

The traditional accompaniments are roast potatoes – which are cooked in hot fat until crisp and brown, approximately 45 minutes to 1 hour depending on size – horseradish sauce and Yorkshire pudding.

Yorkshire Pudding   England

4–5 servings

4 oz plain flour
Pinch salt
1 egg

½ pint milk, or milk and
   water mixed
Knob fat

Sieve the flour with a pinch of salt, beat in the egg and $\frac{1}{2}$ pint milk or milk and water. Allow to stand in a cool place for a while, if wished. Heat a knob of fat in a fairly shallow tin, then pour in the batter and bake towards the top of a hot oven for about 25–30 minutes until well risen, crisp and golden brown.

Apple Dumplings   England

4 servings

12 oz short or sweet shortcrust pastry	4 large cooking apples, peeled and cored
	2 oz sugar

Roll out the pastry, cut into four squares. Put an apple into the centre of each pastry square. Add sugar to taste. Gather the sides of the squares up to completely cover the apple, brush edges with a little water, seal and flute the edges. Put on to a greased tin and bake for approximately 1 hour in the centre of a moderately hot oven.

Christmas Pudding   England

10–16 servings

8 oz cooking apples
12 oz currants
8 oz sultanas
8 oz raisins
4 oz mixed peel
4 oz blanched almonds,
   chopped
8 oz shredded suet
8 oz fresh fine breadcrumbs
4 oz flour

Good pinch salt
$\frac{1}{2}$ teaspoon mixed spice
$\frac{1}{2}$ teaspoon grated nutmeg
8 oz demerara sugar
3 eggs
1 tablespoon golden syrup
Rind and juice $\frac{1}{2}$ lemon
Rind and juice $\frac{1}{2}$ orange
$\frac{1}{4}$ pint sherry or brandy or
   old ale or milk

Peel, and chop or grate apples. Mix all the ingredients together. Stir the mixture well with a wooden spoon. (It is traditional to wish when stirring.) Allow to stand overnight. Turn into a greased 4-pint basin, or two 2-pint basins, and press down pudding mixture. Cover with greased greaseproof paper and pudding cloths or foil and tie down firmly. Boil or steam for 6–7 hours, replenishing water in pan when needed. Remove pudding from pan. Take off damp coverings and cover with clean dry ones making sure the pudding is airtight. Store in a cool dry place until required for use.

   Re-steam for 2–3 hours on Christmas Day. If liked, pour over warmed brandy and ignite. Serve with Brandy Butter (see page 38), custard or fresh cream.

Brandy Butter   England

10–16 servings

4 oz butter   2 tablespoons brandy
5–6 oz icing sugar, sieved

Cream the butter until light and fluffy. Gradually beat in the icing sugar. Add the brandy. Continue beating until the consistency of whipped cream, pile neatly on a small dish and make a pattern, using fork prongs. Serve with Christmas Pudding (see page 37).

Mincemeat   England

Makes 2½ lb

8 oz apples, peeled, cored   2 oz almonds, blanched
  and grated   Little grated nutmeg
8 oz currants   4–6 oz demerara sugar
8 oz raisins   2 tablespoons sherry or
8 oz sultanas   brandy
4 oz candied peel
8 oz suet
Rind and juice of 1½ lemons

Mix all the ingredients together. Pack closely in clean dry jars, cover well and store in a cool dry place. Use for the following recipe.

38

Mince Pies England

12 servings

8 oz short or flaky pastry
10 oz mincemeat
Little caster sugar

Roll out the pastry thinly, cut out twelve 3-inch and twelve 2½-inch rounds, put the 3-inch ones into greased patty tins. Fill with mincemeat. Brush the edges of the pastry with water and place the smaller rounds on top as lids. Seal and flute the edges of the pies, make a small hole in the centre, bake for 15–20 minutes in the centre of a hot oven. Dust with caster sugar.

Treacle Tart England

6–8 servings

6 oz shortcrust pastry
4 oz golden syrup
4 oz black treacle

3 oz breadcrumbs
Rind and juice of ½ lemon

Roll out the pastry and line an 8-inch pie plate or dish. Mix golden syrup, black treacle, breadcrumbs, grated lemon rind and juice together. Fill centre of the plate with the mixture. Roll pastry trimmings, cut into strips and make a pastry lattice. Bake in centre of a moderately hot oven for 30–40 minutes until pastry is pale golden brown. Reduce heat after 15 minutes. Serve with fresh cream or custard.

British Savouries

There are many savoury dishes which are eaten at the end of a meal after a sweet, or in place of a sweet. They are also suitable for supper, high tea or lunch.

Buck Rarebit   British

Top each portion of Welsh rarebit (see page 41) with a poached egg.

Angels on Horseback   British

Wrap a seasoned oyster in half a rasher of bacon; grill the bacon until crisp and brown; serve with hot buttered toast.

Devils on Horseback   British

Wrap one or two stoned cooked prunes in a rasher of bacon; grill the bacon until crisp and brown; serve with hot buttered toast.

Roes on Toast   British

Soften herring roes in a little butter and milk, drain, serve on hot buttered toast topped with paprika.

Mushrooms on Toast   British

Arrange fried mushrooms on hot buttered toast.

Welsh Rarebit   Wales

4–8 servings

1 oz butter	Salt and pepper
1 oz flour	1 teaspoon made mustard
4 tablespoons milk	8 oz Cheddar cheese,
1 tablespoon beer	grated
Worcestershire sauce	4 large pieces buttered
(optional)	toast (or 8 small slices)

Heat the butter, stir in the flour, cook for 1–2 minutes. Add the milk, beer, a few drops Worcestershire sauce, and seasoning, including mustard. Cook until very thick, add the grated Cheddar cheese. Spread on hot buttered toast and grill until golden.

Bara Brith   Wales

12–14 servings

½ oz fresh yeast	4 oz lard
4 oz sugar	2 oz chopped candied peel
½ pint tepid milk	4 oz currants
1 small egg	Pinch mixed spice
1 lb plain flour	6 oz seedless raisins
½ teaspoon salt	

Cream the yeast with a teaspoon of the sugar, add the tepid milk and egg. Sieve flour and salt, rub in lard, add rest of sugar and remaining ingredients. Make a well in the centre, pour in the yeast liquid, sprinkling with a light dusting of flour on top, leave in a warm place for about 20 minutes. After this, mix well, adding extra milk if necessary to give a soft dough. Return to warm place to prove for at least 1 hour. Turn on to a floured board and mix lightly with a warm knife, put into greased and floured 8-inch cake tin, or 2-lb loaf tin, bake for 1–1¼ hours in centre of a moderately hot oven, reduce heat after 30 minutes to very moderate.

Sally Lunns   England

12 servings

1 oz margarine
¼ pint milk
½ oz fresh yeast
1 teaspoon sugar
12 oz flour

Good pinch salt
2 oz sugar
1 egg
1 oz butter, melted

Melt the margarine, add milk and warm to blood heat. Cream the yeast with the teaspoon sugar, then mix into milk mixture. Blend together the flour, salt, and the 2 oz sugar, add yeast liquid together with the beaten egg. Divide into four, knead each piece lightly. Put into small greased and floured cake tins, prick tops lightly, leave to rise to tops of tins. Bake above centre of a moderate oven for 20 minutes. Brush tops with melted butter when cooked. Serve with butter.

Scotch Pancakes Scotland

12 pancakes

4 oz plain flour	1 egg
2 teaspoons baking powder	¼ pint milk
Pinch of salt	1 oz melted margarine
1 oz sugar	(optional)

Make a thick batter with the flour and baking powder, pinch salt, sugar, egg and milk. Lastly, stir in melted margarine (not essential but keeps scones moist). Grease and warm a girdle, griddle, electric hot-plate or frying-pan.

Drop spoons of the batter on to the plate. Cook for about 2 minutes, then turn and cook for a further 2 minutes.

To test whether cooked, press firmly with the back of a knife, and if no batter comes from the sides, and the scones feel firm, cool on a wire sieve; cover with a cloth to keep moist.

Scottish Oaties Scotland

8 oaties

4 oz plain flour	3 oz black treacle
2 level teaspoons baking powder	4 oz butter or margarine
½ level teaspoon salt	Coarse oatmeal or almond nibs
2 oz caster sugar	

Sieve flour, baking powder and salt together. Put caster sugar, black treacle and butter or margarine into a saucepan, heat until just melted. Mix this into flour, stirring well. Press into a greased 7-inch sandwich tin, bake in the centre of a moderate oven for 20 minutes. Sprinkle top with coarse oatmeal or almond nibs. Cut into 8 wedges before mixture cools. Serve with butter for breakfast or tea.

Soda Bread   Ireland

10 slices

½–1 oz margarine
8 oz plain flour
Pinch salt
1 teaspoon bicarbonate of
   soda

¼ pint sour milk or ¼ pint
fresh milk mixed with ½
teaspoon cream of
tartar

To glaze:
A little milk

Rub the margarine into the flour and salt (the margarine is not essential but helps to keep the bread moist). Dissolve the bicarbonate of soda in the sour milk, add to the flour. Knead lightly and form into a round loaf. Brush with a little extra milk and bake on a flat tin in the centre of a very hot oven for 15 minutes. After this time, lower heat to moderately hot for another 10–15 minutes. Serve fresh.

Yorkshire Teacakes England

Makes 5

½ teaspoon sugar
½ pint warm milk
2 level teaspoons dried yeast
   or ½ oz fresh yeast
1 lb plain flour

1 teaspoon salt
1 oz sugar
1 oz lard, melted
2 oz currants
Milk

Blend the sugar with the warm milk, sprinkle on the dried yeast or crumbled fresh yeast. Leave until mixture is covered with bubbles. Blend the flour, salt, sugar, lard and currants with the yeast liquid. Work to a firm dough, adding extra flour if needed. Knead on a floured board for about 5 minutes. Prove for 1½ hours until the dough springs back when pressed lightly with a floured finger. Turn on to the board again and knead. Divide into 5 equal pieces, shape into rounds and roll each out to a circle 6½–7 inches across. Place on a greased baking sheet and brush tops with milk. Prove for 30–45 minutes until almost double in size. Bake in a moderately hot oven for 20 minutes.

Eastern Europe

(Czechoslovakia, Hungary, Poland
and Russia)

Czechoslovakia

Czechoslovakia has a wonderful tradition of satisfying flavoursome food. Sour cream, caraway seeds and mushrooms are used a great deal. Various kinds of dumplings are popular filled with something either savoury or sweet.

Hungary

While similar to Austrian and Czech, Hungarian food tends to be more spicy with greater use made of paprika, onions and sour cream. Some ideas make vegetables and meat both delicious and unusual.

Poland and Russia

Polish food is not unlike Hungarian or Czech. Several of their classic recipes are in this section.

Russian food is gay and colourful with interesting soups and hors d'oeuvres.

Hors d'oeuvres

The most famous of all hors d'oeuvres comes from Russia — it is of course caviare. However, there are much less expensive foods used for hors d'oeuvres.

In both Russia and Poland an excellent start to a meal is the pancake, called Piroshki (see page 52), which can be filled with cooked meat, game, mushrooms in a thick cheese sauce, or cooked fish and hard-boiled eggs.

A pâté not unlike caviare in taste is often made of aubergines in Russia: the halved, seasoned vegetable is cooked until the skins are black, then the centre scooped out and blended with oil, vinegar or lemon juice and salt and pepper to taste.

Potato Soup   Czechoslovakia

Kulajda

4 servings

1 lb potatoes, peeled and diced	2–3 oz mushrooms, diced
Salt and pepper	1 tablespoon flour
1–2 teaspoons caraway seeds	$\frac{1}{2}$ pint single cream
1 medium-sized onion, finely sliced	4 eggs
	1 teaspoon lemon juice or vinegar

Put the potatoes into a saucepan with enough water to cover, add salt and pepper to taste, caraway seeds, and onion. Simmer for 15 minutes, then add the mushrooms. Continue cooking for a

49

further 20 minutes, adding a little more water if necessary. Blend the flour with the cream. Stir into potato mixture. Cook, very slowly so that the mixture does not curdle, stirring gently. Break the eggs into the soup and cook for several minutes so that they set. Finally, stir in a little lemon juice or vinegar and extra salt and pepper to taste.

Cherry Plum Soup   Poland

4 servings

1 lb cherry plums	$\frac{1}{4}$ pint white wine
1$\frac{1}{2}$ pints water	Cinnamon
2 oz sugar	1 oz breadcrumbs
2 tablespoons lemon juice	

Simmer the cherry plums in the water with sugar and lemon juice. When the fruit is tender, sieve and return to the pan with the white wine. Serve sprinkled with cinnamon and a few breadcrumbs.

Apples or cherries can be used instead and flavoured with claret.

Beetroot Soup

Russia

Borshch

4 servings

1 large raw beetroot, peeled	1 stick celery, shredded
8 oz carrots, grated	2 pints stock
1 onion, sliced	2 tablespoons vinegar
1 clove garlic, crushed	2 tablespoons lemon juice
3 tomatoes, skinned and chopped	Salt and pepper
	Sour cream

Grate the beetroot directly into the pan because of the red juice. Add the carrot, onion, garlic, tomatoes and celery. Add the vinegar, lemon juice and season to taste. Simmer until tender – about 1½ hours.

Serve with sour cream.

Potato Pancakes

Poland

Pacuszki z Kartofli

1½ lb potatoes, boiled	Powdered cinnamon
½ pint milk	Sugar to taste
3 eggs	1½ oz butter

Rub the potatoes through a sieve into a basin and mix with the milk, 3 egg yolks, powdered cinnamon and sugar to taste. Beat the egg whites until they are stiff and add to mixture. Beat to a light batter. Fry very thin pancakes in the butter.

Stuffed Pancakes   Poland

Piroshki

4 servings

4 oz flour
Pinch salt
2–3 eggs
½ pint milk
Oil for frying

2–3 oz butter
Salt and pepper
Little paprika (optional)
8 oz cottage cheese, sour
   milk or cream cheese

*Make a batter with the flour, salt, 1–2 eggs and milk, mix well
and use three-quarters to make small pancakes, fry in oil in
the usual way.*

*Blend the butter, remaining egg, salt and pepper and paprika
with the cheese. Put some cheese mixture on each pancake.
Roll up and dip each pancake in the remaining batter, deep fry
in hot oil.*

Cabbage Rissoles   Czechoslovakia

4 servings

1 lb white cabbage, boiled
   and finely chopped
4 oz onions, fried
4 oz mushrooms, fried
2 soft rolls, soaked in milk
2 eggs plus 1 egg, beaten

4 oz smoked ham, chopped
Salt and pepper
1 clove garlic, crushed
Dried breadcrumbs
2 oz lard

Mix together the cabbage, onions and mushrooms. Squeeze surplus milk from the rolls and add bread to cabbage mixture. Add 2 eggs, the ham, salt and pepper to taste and garlic. Mix well, add more bread if too moist. Form into small balls, coat in beaten egg and dried breadcrumbs and fry in hot lard until crisp and brown. Serve with creamed potatoes.

Stuffed Cabbage   Czechoslovakia

4 servings

8 large cabbage leaves	Salt and pepper
1 lb pork, minced	Pinch paprika
2 onions, finely chopped	Pinch powdered ginger
2 oz bacon, chopped	1–2 eggs
3 oz soft breadcrumbs	1 pint stock

Cook the whole cabbage leaves in boiling salted water for a few minutes only, to soften. Mix together the pork, onions, bacon, breadcrumbs, seasoning, paprika and ginger. Bind with the eggs. Divide the mixture between the 8 cabbage leaves and roll up firmly, tying with string if necessary. Put into a dish and cover with the stock. Cover with a lid and cook for one hour in a moderately hot oven.

Cabbage with Cream   Czechoslovakia

4 servings

1 lb cabbage, shredded   Salt and pepper
1 tablespoon vinegar   Caraway seeds
1 tablespoon water   Sour cream

Cook the cabbage for a few minutes in a little boiling salted
water and drain well. Mix together the vinegar and water and
add to the cabbage. Blend together with salt and pepper and
caraway seeds to taste, and sour cream. This is good with hot
or cold meats.

Cabbage Pancakes   Hungary

Batter (see Yorkshire   Paprika
   Pudding, page 35)   Oil
6 oz cabbage, shredded
   and lightly cooked

When the batter is made, add the cabbage and a shake of
paprika. Fry spoonfuls in hot oil until crisp and brown on both
sides.

Green Beans and Cream   Czechoslovakia

4 servings

1 lb cooked, sliced green
  beans
4 oz fried bacon or ham,
  chopped

5-oz carton cultured sour
  cream

Mix all ingredients together and serve cold.
*If no cultured sour cream is available, use fresh cream with
one tablespoon lemon juice added.*

Paprika Mushrooms   Hungary

1 onion, finely chopped
1 oz butter
8–12 oz button mushrooms
1 tablespoon paprika

Salt and pepper
Water
3 tablespoons sour cream

*Fry the onion in butter until soft. Add the mushrooms, paprika,
seasoning and enough water to cover. Simmer gently until
mushrooms are tender and the liquid has evaporated – about
5 minutes. Stir in sour cream, heat through and serve immediately.*

Letscho

2 onions, sliced thinly
Fat
2–3 green peppers

4 tomatoes, skinned and
  sliced
Salt and pepper

Cook the onions in a little hot fat until tender and crisp but not brown. Add the peppers and tomatoes. Season well. Cover the pan and cook gently for about 50 minutes. Serve with meat or fish.

Stuffed Peppers

Hungary

4 servings

4 large or 8 small red or
  green peppers, deseeded
  but kept whole
3–5 onions, chopped
2 oz fat
12 oz minced meat
2–3 oz cooked rice

Salt and pepper
$\frac{1}{2}$ teaspoon chopped dill or
  parsley
1 lb tomatoes, skinned and
  chopped
$\frac{1}{2}$ oz flour
$\frac{1}{4}$ pint cultured sour cream

Blanch the cored peppers in boiling water for 5 minutes. Fry half the onions in half the fat, add the minced meat, rice, salt and pepper, dill or parsley. Stuff the peppers with this mixture.

Meanwhile, prepare the sauce by frying the remaining onions in the remaining fat, then add the tomatoes. Sieve, blend with the flour and return to pan with extra salt and pepper to taste and the sour cream. Add the peppers to the sauce, cover, and simmer gently for about 30 minutes.

If no cultured sour cream is available, use fresh cream with one tablespoon lemon juice added.

Tripe   Poland

Flaki

6 servings

2–2½ lb tripe, well washed
3 oz butter
2 oz flour
3 pints stock
2 carrots, sliced
2 onions, sliced
1 stick of celery, chopped
Bouquet garni

Pinch ginger
Few cloves
Nutmeg
Salt and pepper
Cayenne pepper
Chopped marjoram or
    parsley
Gruyère cheese

Blanch the tripe by bringing to the boil in salted water, drain, wash again in cold water. Put into a saucepan of boiling water and simmer for 5–6 hours. If buying dressed tripe, it only needs blanching, and does not require this earlier cooking. Remove from water and cut into 2-inch lengths. Melt butter in a saucepan, stir in flour, and when brown add the stock with vegetables, mixed herbs, spices and seasoning. Add the tripe, cover and simmer for 2 hours until tender. Serve with chopped marjoram and grated Gruyère cheese.

Chicken Kiev Russia

4 servings

4 spring chickens, boned
   or 4 breast and wing
   portions of larger birds
4 oz butter

1 egg, beaten
Fine breadcrumbs
Oil for deep frying

Bone chickens completely or use breast and wings of larger chickens, removing the tiny bones from the wing. Put a lump of butter into each chicken, roll up firmly. Dip in egg and crumbs and fry in hot oil steadily until golden brown. Drain well and serve with fried parsley, vegetables or salad. Cut through chicken to allow butter to run out.

Hungarian geese are magnificent in flavour – below is a good stuffing used in Hungary which counteracts the richness of the goose.

Stuffing for Goose Hungary

Liver of the goose, chopped
3–4 hard-boiled eggs,
   chopped
4 oz mushrooms, sliced
1 onion, finely chopped

1 tablespoon chopped
   parsley
2 eggs, lightly beaten
2 teaspoons cream
Salt and pepper

Mix together the goose liver, hard-boiled eggs, mushrooms, onion and parsley. Blend with the beaten eggs and cream, and season well to taste.

Stuff into the goose and roast in the usual way, allowing 15 minutes per pound and 15 minutes over (include weight of stuffing) in a hot oven.

Dumplings   Hungary

4–6 servings

Hungarian cooks, like those in Czechoslovakia, enjoy delicious light dumplings, and the following recipe can be served with chicken or goulash.

8 oz plain flour
Pinch of salt
I egg
¼ pint water

I teaspoon oil or melted fat
2 oz melted butter or
   bacon fat

Sieve flour and salt, beat in the egg, water and oil or melted fat. Leave the sticky batter for a time.

Fill a pan with water, bring to the boil, drop small amounts of batter in this and cook for about 10–15 minutes until they rise to the top. Lift out, and serve topped with melted butter or bacon fat.

Goulash

The real Hungarian Goulash is served as a sustaining soup rather than a stew, and is made in the same way as the recipe on page 60 (which has become the more popular dish) with an additional 1½ pints water to give a much more liquid dish. A very few caraway seeds can also be included.

Paprika

Paprika is powdered dried sweet red pepper (capsicum) and is not a hot spice. It gives colour and dryish flavour to many dishes, and is used a great deal as a spice in Eastern Europe – I think it also gives a comfortable feeling to the stomach!

Goulash   Hungary

4–6 servings

2 oz butter
$1\frac{1}{2}$ lb meat, diced
1 lb onions, sliced
Pinch mixed herbs
Salt and pepper
2 tablespoons paprika
Pinch caraway seeds

$\frac{1}{4}$ pint tomato pulp
Stock as needed
1 lb potatoes, peeled and
   sliced
Cultured sour cream
1 tablespoon parsley,
   chopped (optional)

Heat the butter and fry meat in this, add the onions and cook until golden brown. Add herbs, salt and pepper, paprika, caraway seeds and tomato pulp and simmer gently for 30 minutes. Add stock gradually to keep mixture moist. Put in the sliced potatoes, add more tomato pulp if the mixture seems to be drying, then continue cooking very slowly for $1–1\frac{1}{2}$ hours until both meat and potatoes are very tender. During this time, more stock can be added, but a goulash is a very thick stew, so do this gradually. Top with sour cream. Chopped parsley can be added, if liked, for additional colour.

Goulash   Czechoslovakia

Cook as for Hungarian Goulash (see page 60), omitting tomatoes
and paprika. Flavour with pickled cucumbers and moisten
with stock.

Beef Stroganoff   Russia

4 servings

4 thin tender beef steaks,
   cut into strips
Salt and pepper
Pinch mustard
Pinch curry powder
I oz flour
I onion, finely chopped

$1\frac{1}{2}$ oz butter
I pint beef stock
I teaspoon tomato purée
   or I tablespoon tomato
   juice
Sour cream
Brandy (optional)

Season the steak with salt and pepper, mustard and curry
powder. Add flour and onion and fry in the butter, quickly but
without burning. Cover with the stock, add tomato purée or
juice and sour cream. Simmer for about 15 minutes. Flambé
with a little brandy, if liked.

Steak with Garlic   Czechoslovakia

2 servings

2 beef steaks   Salt and pepper
4 cloves of garlic, crushed   Oil

Put the steaks on a plate and press the garlic into both sides of
each steak and season well. Fry or grill using hot oil until
cooked to your liking.

Steak with Capers   Czechoslovakia

4 servings

Salt and pepper   2 teaspoons flour
4 tender beef steaks   2 teaspoons French mustard
2 oz fat   blended with a little water
1 onion, sliced $\frac{1}{4}$ pint sour cream
4 rashers bacon, chopped   1–2 tablespoons capers

Season the steaks well on both sides and fry in a little hot fat
together with the onion and bacon. Remove and keep hot.
Add the flour, mustard, sour cream and capers to the pan.
Stir and heat together gently. Return the steaks to this sauce
and cook for a minute only to warm through. Serve immediately.

Veal in Pepper Cream Sauce   Czechoslovakia

4 servings

12 oz–1 lb veal fillet, diced
2 oz butter
2 onions, chopped
Salt and pepper

Paprika blended with a
    little water
½ pint sour cream

Fry the veal in the butter together with the onions. Add seasoning to taste, the paprika and cover with sour cream. Continue cooking gently until the veal is tender.

Veal in Batter   Czechoslovakia

4 servings

4 thin slices of veal
Batter (see page 34)

Grated cheese (optional)

Coat the veal with batter which can be flavoured with grated cheese if liked. Fry steadily until crisp and brown.

Pork with Caraway Seeds   Czechoslovakia

4 servings

4 pork cutlets or chops
Seasoned flour
1 oz fat for frying
Water or stock
Caraway seeds to taste

2 tomatoes, sliced (optional)
1 green or red pepper,
  deseeded and diced
  (optional)

Coat the pork with seasoned flour. Fry in a little fat until nearly
cooked. Stir in a little water or stock and the caraway seeds.
Continue cooking until this has made a thick sauce. If liked, add
the vegetables at the same time as the water or stock.

Plum Dumplings   Czechoslovakia

4 servings

4 oz butter
2 eggs
Pinch salt
6 oz cottage cheese or
  curd cheese
5 oz breadcrumbs
2 oz semolina

2 oz flour
2 oz sugar
8–12 plums, stoned
8–12 lumps sugar
Cinnamon
Caster sugar

Blend 2 oz butter with the eggs, salt and cheese. Fry breadcrumbs
in 1 oz butter, then add to the butter mixture together with the
semolina, flour and sugar. The dough should be a pliable
consistency; if too firm add a little milk; if too soft add a little

more flour. Divide into small flat round pieces, put a plum on each round. Put a lump of sugar into each plum, and a shake of cinnamon. Mould the dough carefully round the plums and poach in boiling water for approximately 7–8 minutes; they rise when ready.

Lift out of the water, sprinkle with sugar. Melt remaining butter and pour over dumplings. Serve while hot.

Rich Chocolate Gâteau   Poland

Tort Kosciuszko

10–12 servings

4 eggs	1 teaspoon rum or brandy
4 oz caster sugar	4 oz plain chocolate
4 oz ground almonds	1 tablespoon black coffee
4 oz melted chocolate	$\frac{1}{2}$ oz butter
$\frac{1}{2}$ pint cream	

Put the eggs and sugar into a large bowl and whisk until thick. Fold in the almonds and melted chocolate. Put three-quarters of this mixture into a greased sandwich tin in a very moderate oven and cook for 45 minutes. Put remainder into a smaller greased tin to use for crumbs. Bake for 25 minutes above centre of oven.

Turn out both cakes, cool and store for 24 hours.

Make fine crumbs of smaller cake. Whip the cream and the rum or brandy, add the cake crumbs and spread over the larger cake. Melt the plain chocolate with the coffee and butter. Cool, then spoon over the cream-topped cake, leaving a little cream showing.

65

France

France

French food is renowned all over the world for classic simplicity and superb sauces. The French are internationally recognized as masters of the art of cooking. The reason behind this is historical and goes back to the time of Louis XIV and the French Empire, when the Court was supremely interested in food. The best chefs in the world were brought there to create dishes which remain in the classic French repertoire.

Soups in France

The French make a great variety of soups, from satisfying cream soups to the more sophisticated clear consommé. One of the most famous French soups is Bouillabaisse (fish soup). This is not particularly easy to make at home due to the wide variety of fish needed. In parts of France the fish are bought alive and freshly killed for this dish. The recipe varies according to the area of France, but this is my favourite version.

Bouillabaisse France

4–6 servings

Selection of prepared fish
and shellfish (allow ½ lb
per head)
2 onions, sliced
2 cloves garlic, crushed
4 tomatoes, skinned and
sliced

3 tablespoons olive oil
Pinch saffron
Little chopped fennel
2 bay leaves
Salt and pepper
Chopped parsley

*Choose several kinds of white fish, plus prawns or lobster or
some kind of shellfish. Fry the onions, garlic and tomatoes in the
olive oil. Flavour with saffron, fennel and bay leaves. Chop the
fish, and add the vegetables with salt and pepper and enough
boiling water to cover (you can use a mixture of wine and water
if liked). Cook for about 10 minutes. Lift out the pieces of fish, put
into soup plates with toasted or oven-dried French bread, strain the
liquid over the fish and garnish with chopped parsley.*

Mussels France

Moules à la Marinière

4–6 servings

2–3 pints mussels
Salt and pepper
2 onions, finely chopped
2 oz butter

3 tomatoes, skinned and
chopped
Bouquet garni
½ pint water

First, prepare the mussels by scrubbing them well and rinsing in several changes of salted water. Discard all open shells.

Fry the onions gently for 10 minutes in butter. Add the tomatoes and herbs. Cover pan, cook for 15 minutes.

In another large wide pan put $\frac{1}{2}$ pint water and the mussels. Place a tea towel wrung out in boiling water on top of them, leave for 2–3 minutes over fierce heat until their shells open. Remove one shell from each pair. Strain the mussel liquor into the onion and tomato mixture, add mussels, plenty of pepper and heat gently through. If the mixture looks too thin for your taste, thicken it by adding some soft white breadcrumbs, but do not use flour.

Moules à la Marinière (variation)

4 servings

4 pints mussels
1 onion, chopped
1 clove garlic, crushed
2 oz butter

Bouquet garni
$\frac{1}{4}$ pint white wine
Parsley

Clean the mussels as in recipe above. Fry the onion and garlic in the butter for a few minutes. Add the mussels, herbs and white wine. Cook, covered, for about 5 minutes. Stir in the parsley and serve.

Crab Soufflé

France

Soufflé en Crabe

4 servings

1 oz butter	Salt and pepper
1 oz flour	Little paprika
¼ pint milk	6 oz crabmeat
3 eggs	

In a large pan, make a thick sauce with the butter, flour and milk. Cool a little, stir in the beaten egg yolks, salt, pepper and paprika. Add the flaked crabmeat and fold in stiffly beaten egg whites. Put in buttered soufflé dish and bake in centre of moderate oven for 25–30 minutes until risen and brown. Serve at once.

Variations

Cheese Soufflé

Substitute 3–4 oz grated cheese in place of crabmeat.

Spinach Soufflé

Use thick spinach purée plus 3 tablespoons cream in place of milk. Omit crabmeat.

71

Bacon and Cheese Flan   France

Quiche Lorraine

4 servings

6 oz shortcrust pastry
2–3 rashers rindless bacon
2 eggs
½ pint milk or ¼ pint milk
  and ¼ pint cream

6 oz Gruyère cheese,
  grated or sliced
Salt and pepper

Line a deep 7-inch flan ring with the pastry, pressing down well. Chop bacon and fry lightly. Beat eggs, add milk or milk and cream, grated or sliced cheese, bacon and seasoning to taste. Pour into pastry case, bake in centre of a hot oven for 15 minutes, lower the heat to moderate for a further 30 minutes.

Celeriac Salad   France

Céleri-rave Remoulade

4 servings

1 large celeriac root
2 tablespoons olive oil
1 tablespoon wine vinegar
½ teaspoon salt and pepper
Remoulade sauce:
Yolks of 2 hard-boiled eggs

1 raw egg yolk
½–1 tablespoon made
  mustard
½ pint olive oil
1 tablespoon wine vinegar

Cut up the celeriac root into tiny matchsticks. (It tends to look a little like an unattractive turnip, but the flavour is delicious.) Mix together the oil, vinegar, salt and pepper and pour over the sticks. Allow to soak for several hours, then cover with the sauce which is made as follows.

Cream the yolks of the hard-boiled eggs with the raw egg yolk and the mustard. Add the olive oil, drop by drop, stirring all the time. When all the oil has been added, stir the wine vinegar into the sauce.

Salad from Nice   France

Salade Niçoise

4 servings

8 oz cooked potatoes, diced
8 oz cooked green beans, sliced
3 tablespoons olive oil
1½ tablespoons white wine vinegar

Salt and pepper
4 tomatoes, quartered
8 anchovy fillets
8 black olives, stoned
Chopped chervil
Chopped tarragon

Put the potatoes and beans into a salad bowl. Blend together the olive oil, vinegar and salt and pepper to taste. Toss the vegetables in this. Garnish with the tomatoes, anchovy fillets, stoned black olives and a little chopped chervil and tarragon. If liked, the salad can be served on a bed of lettuce.

Marrow and Vegetable Stew   France
Ratatouille

4–8 servings

1 lb tomatoes, skinned and halved
Salt and pepper
Bacon fat or little oil
2 onions, chopped
1–2 cloves garlic, crushed

1 medium-sized marrow, peeled and cut in chunks
4 small aubergines, cut in chunks
1 green or red pepper, deseeded and sliced
Chopped parsley

Sprinkle tomatoes with salt and leave to drain. Heat fat or oil in a heavy pan and gently fry onions and crushed garlic. Add tomatoes, marrow, aubergines, and green or red pepper. Season well with salt and pepper and simmer slowly, with well-fitting lid on pan, until vegetables are tender. Serve garnished with parsley.

This can be served as a separate course or with the main dish.

Chicken Marengo   France
Poulet à la Marengo

4 servings

1 young chicken, skinned and jointed
Little seasoned flour
3 tablespoons oil or mixture butter and oil
1 onion, chopped
1 clove garlic, crushed

8 oz tomatoes, chopped and skinned
1 small can tomato purée
½ pint white wine or chicken stock or mixture stock and wine
4 tablespoons sherry
4 oz button mushrooms

Get your butcher to prepare the chicken. Coat in seasoned flour. Fry in hot oil until golden, remove from pan. Add onion and garlic, fry lightly, then add the tomatoes. Continue cooking for 5 minutes. Add the tomato purée, wine or stock, sherry and mushrooms. Replace chicken pieces, cover pan and simmer for 20–30 minutes or until the chicken is tender.

For a more elaborate dish, pieces of lobster can be added during the last 5–10 minutes of cooking, and each serving can be topped with a fried egg.

Beef Bourguignonne   France

Boeuf à la Bourguignonne

8–10 servings

This is a cook-it-yourself-at-the-table dish. Good for leisurely dinner parties.

8 oz butter
$\frac{1}{2}$ pint oil
$1\frac{1}{2}$–2 lb fillet or tender
  rump steak, cut in cubes

Selection of sauces (see
    page 76)

Bring the butter and oil to the boil – keep bubbling over a low heat – in a fondue pan if you have one or a deep pan. Spear a piece of steak with a fork and immerse in the hot oil and cook about 1 minute. Dip into Hollandaise, Béarnaise or Tartare Sauce and serve with crisp French bread.

This name is also given to a delicious beef casserole where meat and vegetables are cooked in red Burgundy. Brown steak in hot oil, add a few shallots, a crushed clove of garlic, and shake of seasoned flour. Cover in wine; simmer until tender.

Hollandaise Sauce   France

3 egg yolks
Pinch cayenne pepper
Salt and pepper

1–2 tablespoons lemon juice
  or white vinegar
2–3 oz butter

*Put the egg yolks, pinch cayenne, salt and pepper into a basin.
Add lemon juice or white vinegar and whisk until thick over a pan
of hot water. Gradually whisk in butter.*

Tartare sauce: *make Hollandaise sauce, add a mixture of
finely chopped parsley, capers and gherkins. Alternatively, mix
the parsley, capers and gherkins into mayonnaise.*

Béarnaise sauce: *make Hollandaise sauce with the addition of
chopped parsley and a finely chopped shallot.*

Chicken Casserole   France

Poulet en Cocotte Bonne Femme

4–6 servings

Liver from chicken, diced
8 oz pork sausagemeat
Pinch mixed herbs
1 large roasting chicken
1 oz butter
1 tablespoon oil
2 sticks celery, diced
Celery leaves

2 turnips, diced
6 carrots, diced
Salt and pepper
2 bay leaves
Bouquet garni
1 pint stock
4–6 potatoes, diced
Little cream (optional)

Blend the diced chicken liver with sausagemeat and herbs, stuff into the chicken, then brown outside of bird in the butter and oil until golden. Add remaining ingredients except potatoes and cream. Cover the pan tightly, simmer gently for $1\frac{1}{4}$–$1\frac{1}{2}$ hours. Add the finely diced potatoes and continue cooking for a further 30–45 minutes. Put chicken on to a dish with all the vegetables except the potatoes. Remove the herbs from stock and beat the potatoes into the stock to form a sauce, adding a little cream and extra seasoning if required.

This dish can be varied by adding fat bacon, mushrooms, onions or other vegetables in season.

Rum Omelette   France

Omelette Flambée

3–4 servings

4 eggs	Unsalted butter
2 tablespoons water	Caster sugar
Salt	Warm rum

Beat 4 egg yolks until thick and lemon coloured, beat in 2 tablespoons water and pinch salt. Beat 4 egg whites until stiff, and fold into yolk mixture. Heat a little butter in large omelette pan with heatproof handle, pour in omelette mixture. Cook mixture over low heat until fluffy and lightly browned on bottom, about 5 minutes. Finish in slow oven until golden brown, about 12–15 minutes. Loosen and slide on to warm dish. Spread with choice of filling. Fold and sprinkle with caster sugar and just before serving, sprinkle with warm rum and ignite.

Suggested fillings:
(a) *Hot redcurrant jelly*
(b) *Hot apricots and blanched almonds*
(c) *Poached apple slices mixed with apricot jam and rum*
(d) *Crumbled macaroon biscuits and maraschino cherries*

Chestnut Sweet

France

Mont Blanc

3–4 servings

1 lb chestnuts
Water

2 oz sugar
Little vanilla essence

Wash the chestnuts. Split their skins, and simmer for 10 minutes, then remove skins while warm. Return to pan with a little water, the sugar and vanilla essence and cook for 10 minutes. Sieve, then pipe thin threads of the purée to form a pyramid. Serve with cream.

Canned unsweetened chestnut purée can be used instead.

Chocolate Mousse

France

Mousse au Chocolat

4 servings

4 oz plain chocolate
4 eggs
2 oz sugar

2 tablespoons brandy
Whipped cream

Break the chocolate into squares and put into a basin over hot water. Stir until just soft. Add the egg yolks and sugar, beat until thick. Fold in brandy and beat again for another 2 minutes. Take the basin off the heat, whisk until cold, fold in stiffly beaten egg whites. Divide between 4 glasses and chill.

Top with whipped cream just before serving.

Cheese Aigrettes   France

Aigrettes au Fromage

2 tablespoons water	3 oz Parmesan cheese,
I oz butter	grated
2 oz flour	Salt and pepper
2 eggs	Oil for deep frying

Heat the water and butter together. Add the flour and dry over low heat as Choux Pastry (see recipe below). Gradually beat in eggs, I½ oz cheese and salt and pepper to taste. Drop teaspoons of mixture into hot oil, fry for about 7 minutes until crisp and brown, drain and serve sprinkled with remaining grated cheese.

Choux Pastry   France

Pâté Choux

¼ pint water	3 oz plain or self-raising
I oz margarine	flour
Pinch of sugar	2 eggs plus I egg yolk, well
	beaten

Put water, margarine and sugar in a saucepan. Heat gently until margarine and sugar have melted. Stir in the flour. Return pan to low heat, cook very gently but thoroughly, stirring all the time, until mixture is dry enough to form a ball, leaving pan clean. Remove pan from heat, cool, and gradually beat in eggs. Do this slowly to produce a perfectly smooth mixture. Use for the following:

79

Cream Buns

8 servings

Put choux pastry mixture into piping bag and force through large plain pipe on to greased and floured baking trays, or put spoons of mixture into greased and floured patty tins.

Bake in centre of hot oven for 15 minutes, then reduce heat to moderately hot for 20 minutes. The buns should now be pale golden in colour, but feel firm and crisp. Cool gradually, away from any draught. When buns are quite cold, split them and fill with cream. Cover with sieved icing sugar.

Choux pastry can also be used for Churros (see page 135).

Italy

Italy

Italian food is varied and tasty – herbs are used a great deal. Some of their most famous dishes are Minestrone Soup (see page 84), Spaghetti Bolognese (see page 86), Ice Cream (see page 93), and Zabaglione (see page 95). Their great artistic ability and imagination are shown in their presentation of food which always looks appetizing.

Use of Herbs in Italian Cooking

Herbs are often used in dishes – see Pizza, page 87. Oregano is wild marjoram and is used in salads as well as many meat dishes.

Sage is added to veal to give one of the most delicious Italian meat dishes – Saltimbocca, thin slices of veal seasoned and coated with chopped sage, then fried in butter, and finally topped with ham before serving.

Garlic is used sparingly in soups, savoury dishes and salads.

Another Italian herb is Florence fennel, which is used in two ways. The base is sliced and added to salads, where it looks like sliced celery, but has an aniseed taste. The feathery leaves can be put into sauces to serve with fish.

Italian vegetable dishes are both colourful and full of flavour – they can be a complete course in themselves, or served with meat or fish. The following are examples of these.

Hors d'oeuvres

Antipasto   Italy

These can vary a great deal from a small portion of pasta to a simple cold dish or selection of cold dishes such as the following:
Vegetables: sliced peppers, sliced fennel, sliced celery, grated raw carrot mixed with cooked rice, sliced tomatoes and olives.
Fish: tuna fish, sardines, anchovies, small portions white, shellfish, octopus and mussels, coated in batter and fried.
Meat: sliced salami, sliced ham, garnished with fresh sliced vegetables.

S–WC–E   83

Minestrone

4 servings

One of the most famous of Italian soups is Minestrone, which can be substantial enough for a main course.

3 oz white haricot beans
$1\frac{1}{2}$ pints water or white stock
1 large onion, finely chopped
2 tablespoons olive oil
1 clove garlic, crushed
1–2 oz bacon, diced
1 stick celery, chopped

8 oz fresh or canned tomatoes
1 large carrot, diced
8 oz cabbage, finely shredded
2 oz short macaroni
Salt and pepper
Chopped parsley
Grated Parmesan cheese

Soak haricot beans overnight in the water or stock.

Toss onion in hot oil with crushed garlic and bacon. Add haricot beans and their liquid. Simmer gently for about $1\frac{1}{2}$ hours. Add all remaining vegetables except cabbage. Cook for a further 20 minutes, adding a little more water if necessary. Add cabbage and macaroni, cook until both are just tender. Add salt and pepper to taste. Serve garnished with parsley and cheese. A little red wine can be used in this recipe.

Ways to use pasta

For a simple dish, boil in plenty of salted water and toss in butter and cheese or just toss in butter and use as a vegetable. Mix with oil and vinegar and serve in a salad, or mix with a sauce as an hors d'oeuvre or main dish.

Types of pasta	Ways to serve
CANNELLONI – looks like huge tubes of macaroni	Generally stuffed and served with tomato or cheese sauce
FARFALLE – bows of all sizes	With butter and parsley, in a sauce or salad
FETTUCCINE – long, wide egg noodles	As noodles or lasagne (see page 87)
FIDELINI – finest spaghetti, comes twirled into a nest	Often used fried or served with butter and chopped parsley
FUSILLI – like macaroni only twisted	As macaroni
GNOCCHI – often made at home – the true gnocchi is a dumpling shape of pasta or potato	With cheese or cheese sauce
LASAGNE – wide ribbons of pasta - there is plain lasagne or a green (spinach-flavoured) lasagne. A narrow ribbon is Tagliatelle	This gives its name to a casserole dish (see page 87)
LINGUINE – flat ribbon-like pasta	Toss in butter and parsley, often served with fish
MACCHERONI – which we call macaroni. There is thick macaroni and a shorter, quick-cooking, elbow-length variety. This is also the name given to all pasta with a hole in the centre	In a cheese sauce such as macaroni cheese. In milk puddings as other pasta
MARUZZE – large shell macaroni	As macaroni
NOODLES – generally the name given to pasta which has egg added, various shapes	As other pasta of similar shape – used in Chinese cookery

RAVIOLI – one of the most popular pasta foods – squares of pasta filled with a meat or vegetable stuffing	Served with tomato or cheese sauce – available canned
RIGATONI – rather like cannelloni or large macaroni, ribbed down the outside	As cannelloni
SEMINI – tiny seedlike pasta	In soups
SPAGHETTI – the most popular form of pasta for savoury dishes in this country, long thin sticks	Use with a variety of sauces
VERMICELLI – like very fine spaghetti	In soups or use in place of spaghetti

Spaghetti with Meat Sauce   Italy

Spaghetti Bolognese

4–6 servings

1 oz butter	Salt and pepper
1 tablespoon olive oil	$\frac{1}{2}$ pint good stock if using canned tomatoes, slightly more for tomato purée
2 oz mushrooms, finely chopped	
1 onion, shredded	
1 carrot, shredded	$\frac{1}{4}$ pint red wine
4–6 oz minced raw beef	6 oz spaghetti
1 small can tomatoes or tomato purée	Parmesan cheese, grated

Cook the sauce first as it takes longer than the spaghetti.
Heat the butter and oil in a pan and gently fry the mushrooms, onion and carrot for a few minutes. Stir in minced beef, simmer gently, then add rest of ingredients, except the spaghetti and

86

cheese. Continue to cook, stirring from time to time until sauce thickens and has a rich flavour. Cook the spaghetti in boiling salted water until just tender – about 10–15 minutes. Drain spaghetti. Serve the spaghetti on a hot dish, top with the sauce and sprinkle with grated cheese.

Lasagne   Italy

4 servings

Make the meat sauce for Spaghetti Bolognese (see page 86). Cook 8 oz lasagne in boiling salted water; drain and allow to dry. Arrange a layer of the pasta, a layer of meat sauce, and a layer of Ricotta (cream cheese), Mozzarella (a firm cheese) and grated Parmesan (the strong cooking cheese). Continue to fill the dish like this but end with Parmesan cheese. Bake for about 40 minutes in a moderate oven.

Tomato Pie   Italy
Pizza

6–8 servings

8 oz plain flour	$2\frac{1}{2}$-oz can tomato purée
1 level teaspoon salt	1 teaspoon sugar
$\frac{1}{2}$ oz fresh yeast	Salt and pepper
$\frac{1}{4}$ pint lukewarm milk	1 bay leaf
1 small egg	Pinch oregano
1 oz butter, softened	Small can anchovy fillets
$\frac{1}{2}$ oz vegetable cooking fat	1 oz cheese, grated or
or 1 tablespoon oil	sliced
1 small onion, chopped	4–6 olives
8 oz tomatoes*	

*Use skinned fresh tomatoes with 2 tablespoons water, or canned tomatoes.

Sieve the flour and salt. Cream the yeast with a little warm milk, add the egg and the rest of the milk. Add gradually to flour, blend in softened butter. Beat well with the hand until mixture comes away from fingers, return to bowl. Cover with a cloth, leave to prove for 40 minutes in a warm place.

Melt the fat and fry the onion until tender and golden. Add the tomatoes, tomato purée, sugar, seasoning, bay leaf and oregano. Simmer for 10–15 minutes, until the mixture is thick. Cool.

Grease a large baking tray. Pat out dough to about a 9-inch round – put on baking tray. Cover with filling to within $\frac{1}{2}$ inch of edge, then top with washed anchovies, cheese and olives.

Prove for about 15 minutes in a warm place, then bake for about 25–30 minutes in the centre of a hot oven. Serve hot or cold.

Risotto   Italy

4 servings

This is a dish based on rice, and there are many variations of the rest of the ingredients. Here is just one example.

2 onions, sliced	$1\frac{1}{2}$ pints chicken stock
3 tomatoes, sliced	Salt and pepper
2 oz mushrooms	6 oz chicken livers, diced
2 tablespoons olive oil	1 oz sultanas
6 oz long-grain rice	Grated Parmesan cheese

Fry the onions, tomatoes and mushrooms in the oil. Add rice, chicken stock, and salt and pepper to taste. Cook for 15 minutes. Add chicken livers and sultanas. Continue cooking until liquid is absorbed. Serve with grated Parmesan cheese sprinkled on top.

Fricassée of Artichokes   Italy

Carciofi in Fricassea

4 servings

4 globe artichokes	I tablespoon lemon juice
I oz butter	Water
I clove garlic, crushed	I oz grated Parmesan
2 egg yolks	cheese

*Remove outer leaves from the artichokes and simmer artichoke
hearts in boiling salted water for about 30 minutes, then drain.
Heat the butter and garlic together in a pan, add artichokes and
cover tightly. Simmer for a further 30 minutes, do not let it burn.
Add a very little water if the pan appears to be boiling dry.
Beat egg yolks with lemon juice, 2 tablespoons water and the
cheese. Stir into artichoke mixture, which by this time will have
become very soft and cook slowly for about 10 minutes.*

Stuffed Aubergines   Italy

Melanzane Ripiene

4 servings

4 aubergines, halved	Little milk
I onion, chopped	2 slices bread
4 oz mushrooms	4 oz ham, chopped
2 tomatoes, skinned	Salt and pepper
3 oz butter	

Remove flesh from aubergines, reserve skins. Fry the onion, mushrooms, and tomatoes in 2 oz butter. Pour a little milk over the bread, soak for a few minutes and squeeze dry. Add to the onion mixture. Stir in the ham and aubergines' flesh, season well. Pile into aubergine cases, top with remaining butter. Bake for approximately 1 hour in a very moderate oven.

Stuffed Small Baby Marrows   Italy

Zucchine Ripiene

4 servings

1 lb zucchini or small marrows	1 tablespoon oil
1 onion, chopped	4 oz minced beef, cooked
1 clove garlic, crushed	Salt and pepper
4 tomatoes, skinned and chopped	2 oz breadcrumbs
	2 oz cheese, grated

Wash, but do not peel the zucchini or small marrows. Either simmer zucchini whole in boiling water or steam them for approximately 10 minutes, until tender but not overcooked. Cut into halves lengthways through centre. Scoop out pulp. The seeds are so young they need not be discarded. Chop pulp and mix with onion, garlic and tomatoes. Fry in 1 tablespoon oil until tender.

Add the minced beef and season well. Put halves of zucchini on to a greased baking tin. Fill with mixture. Top with breadcrumbs and grated cheese and cook for 15 minutes in moderately hot oven.

Rice Salad   Italy

4 servings

8 oz rice
2 green peppers, shredded
4 tomatoes, peeled and
  sliced
1 aubergine, sliced

2 tablespoons oil
3 tablespoons French
  dressing
2 oz ham, diced (optional)

Cook rice in plenty of boiling, salted water until just soft,
about 15 minutes. Rinse in cold water and drain.
  Fry the peppers, tomatoes and aubergine in the oil until soft.
Add the cooked rice and stir over a low heat for a few minutes.
Put French dressing in a bowl.
  Add rice and vegetables and toss well. Serve chilled. Just before
serving, garnish with little diced ham, if liked.

Veal Stew   Italy

Ossobuco

4 servings

1½–2 lb stewing veal, cut
  into neat pieces, or 3 lb
  knuckle of veal
1 oz flour mixed with salt
  and pepper
3 onions, sliced
1 oz butter
1 tablespoon oil
3 carrots, diced
1 stick celery, chopped

3 tomatoes, skinned and
  chopped
Bouquet garni
Salt and pepper
Grated rind and juice of
  1 lemon
½ pint dry white wine
1 tablespoon concentrated
  tomato purée
½ pint water
Chopped parsley

Roll meat in the seasoned flour. Fry onions in hot butter and oil until pale golden. Add the meat, carrots, celery, tomatoes, herbs and seasoning. Toss with onions for 2–3 minutes. Stir in lemon rind and juice, wine and tomato purée diluted with the water. Simmer for 2 hours. Remove meat and keep warm, remove bag of herbs. Rub sauce through sieve, pour over meat and garnish with chopped parsley.

If liked, this can be served with boiled rice, topped with melted butter and grated cheese.

Fruit Dishes

In season wonderful peaches, figs, apricots and plums abound in Italy, and are often served as they are, fresh off the trees. Sometimes they are coated with a thin batter and fried as fritters.

Peaches are sometimes stuffed with crumbled macaroon biscuits mixed with chopped almonds, and bound with an egg yolk, then baked in the oven for a short time.

Genoese Tart   Italy

Torta Genovese

6–8 servings

4 oz puff pastry	½ teaspoon vanilla essence
2 oz butter	Apricot jam
3 oz sugar	4 oz icing sugar
3 oz blanched almonds, chopped	Juice of ½ lemon
3 eggs	Water

Line the sides of a pie dish with the pastry. Cream the butter and sugar until soft, add chopped almonds, egg yolks and vanilla essence, and lastly fold in the stiffly beaten egg whites. Pour into the lined pie dish and bake for about 15 minutes in the centre of a hot oven, lower the heat to moderate for further 15–20 minutes.

Top with apricot jam. Blend 4 oz icing sugar with juice of $\frac{1}{2}$ lemon and a little water if necessary. Spread over top of the tart. Serve cold.

Ice Cream   Italy

Gelato

4 servings

2 eggs $\frac{1}{2}$ pint evaporated milk,
$\frac{1}{2}$ pint milk   or single cream, lightly
2 oz sugar   whipped
Little vanilla essence

Always turn the cold control indicator of the refrigerator to the coldest position at least $\frac{1}{2}$ hour before freezing. Turn indicator to normal setting to store the ice cream. If you have a 2- or 3-star marking on your refrigerator or own a home freezer there is no need to alter the normal setting to freeze the ice cream.

Cook egg yolks and milk slowly in a double saucepan until a thick custard. Allow to cool. Meanwhile, stiffly beat egg whites. Add sugar and flavourings, lightly whipped evaporated milk or cream and stiffly beaten egg whites to custard. Freeze on coldest setting until lightly set. Whip to aerate; re-freeze.

Variations to the basic vanilla ice cream can be made as follows, omitting the vanilla essence.

Fruit ice cream: *add about* $\frac{1}{4}$ – $\frac{1}{2}$ *pint thick sweetened fruit purée.*
Coffee ice cream: *add 1–2 tablespoon coffee essence.*
Chocolate ice cream: *add 2–3 oz chocolate powder or melted chocolate.*
Tutti-frutti ice cream: *add diced glacé cherries, nuts and candied peel.*

Ice Cream Gâteau

Italy

Cassata

Make up the basic ice-cream custard (see page 93) and divide into three. Add vanilla essence to one-third, fruit flavour to a second and a chocolate or tutti-frutti to the final third. Let each ice cream half-set.

Take out the vanilla, pack round the side of a mould. Pack the fruit flavour next. Add the chocolate or tutti-frutti in the centre.

Freeze in the mould until firm. For successful results, the ice creams must be sufficiently frozen to stay in position.

Milk Pudding

Italy

4 servings

3 oz soft bread
Little boiling water
2–3 oz blanched almonds,
  finely chopped

1 pint milk
4 eggs

94

Moisten the bread in a little boiling water, squeeze dry. Blend the almonds with the bread, add to the milk. Simmer gently until it is a smooth mixture, stirring constantly. Blend with the eggs. Put into greased dish and bake for I hour in a slow oven. Serve hot with fruit purée or Zabaglione.

Zabaglione   Italy

4 servings

4 egg yolks
4 oz caster sugar
4–8 tablespoons Marsala

Put egg yolks and caster sugar into a large bowl over hot water, and whisk until thick and frothy.

Gradually whisk in the Marsala and continue whisking until very light and thick. Pour into glasses and serve with sponge fingers or crisp biscuits, or with Milk Pudding (see above).

Middle East,
Mediterranean
and North Africa

Middle East, Mediterranean and North Africa

It is unusual to group a vast range of countries together, for each has its own traditions, but the food of the countries of the Middle East, most of which border the Mediterranean, have certain things in common in their tasty use of herbs and spices, vegetables, lamb, mutton and yoghourt.

Leek Soup   Greece

Finely sliced leeks are cooked in well-seasoned water or
clear chicken stock, then the liquid thickened slightly with
cornflour, and lemon juice and oil to taste added.

Cucumber and Yoghourt Soup   Iran

4 servings

4 spring onions, finely
   chopped
½ tablespoon chopped mint
½ tablespoon chopped
   summer savory
1 teaspoon chopped basil

1 pint yoghourt
1 cucumber, peeled and
   diced
Salt and pepper
Chopped walnuts

*Mix the spring onions and the herbs with 1 pint yoghourt, then
blend with the cucumber and plenty of seasoning. Serve cold,
topped with chopped walnuts.*

Hors d'oeuvres

*Dolmas made with vine leaves (see page 100), are an excellent
first course.
Plates of olives – black and green are popular in Greece.
Turkish or Istanbul eggs – for which eggs are boiled in equal
quantities of olive oil, Turkish coffee (see page 117) and onion*

skins. Boil for some hours. Serve cold. The eggs have a delicious nutty taste.

Salted cod's roe, blended with crushed garlic and butter, makes an excellent pâté – popular in Turkey and Greece – served with salad. Taramasalata is generally the name given. Tamara is the title when mullet's roe is substituted for cod's roe.

Israeli menus often begin with fruit juices, rollmop herrings, egg salads or chopped liver.

Stuffed Vine Leaves   Turkey

Dolmas

6 servings

1 large onion, chopped	Pinch chopped fresh mint or dried mint
3 tablespoons olive oil	Salt and pepper
6 tablespoons uncooked rice	Pinch cinnamon
4 tablespoons pine kernels or shredded almonds	About 30 vine leaves (must be young leaves)
12 oz minced beef	$\frac{1}{4}$ pint white wine
	Water

Fry onion in the hot oil for a few minutes, then add the rice and fry gently until pale golden. Add nuts and cook for 1 minute. Remove from the heat, add the meat, mint, salt and pepper and cinnamon. Mix well.

Dip the vine leaves for 1 minute in hot water to tenderize them. Remove with a perforated spoon. Spread the vine leaves out flat, and put a tablespoon of the meat mixture in the centre of each. Fold in the ends, and roll into finger shapes.

Put rolls into a pan, cover with the wine, add water, if necessary, to cover the leaves, for they must not be left dry at beginning. Cook for about 25 minutes, covered, over a low heat, then remove lid so the liquid gradually evaporates. Serve hot or cold. They are generally served as an hors d'oeuvre.

Bastilla   Morocco

4–8 servings

This can be a main dish or an hors d'oeuvre.

True bastilla is a most complicated pastry. The dough, while being made with just flour and water, is cooked in such a way on flat plates, that it becomes wafer thin. This needs practice and also the correct large flat plate for cooking. But frozen or home-made puff pastry, rolled out paper thin, can be used instead.

2 pigeons
2–4 oz butter
¾ pint water
Pinch salt
1 onion, finely chopped
Pinch ginger
Pinch saffron
Small piece chopped chilli
   (hot pepper)

1 teaspoon chopped
   parsley
Pinch powdered coriander
   or ginger
2–4 eggs
1–2 oz sugar
2 oz chopped blanched
   almonds
Pinch powdered cinnamon
1 lb puff pastry

Fry the pigeons for a few minutes in the butter. Add the water, salt, onion, ginger, saffron, chilli, parsley and coriander or ginger. Cover and simmer slowly for 1 hour. Drain, remove all

101

meat from the bones, chopping it very finely and discard bones. Divide the stock in half. Beat half into the eggs, and cook until lightly set, as scrambled egg. Use the other half of the stock for a gravy to serve with the pasties if required. Mix together the sugar, almonds and cinnamon. Roll out pastry until paper thin; cut into 12 rounds. Put the first round on the table, sprinkle with a quarter of the sugar mixture.

Cover with second layer of pastry, then a layer of pigeon meat and egg, top with pastry. Seal edges very firmly, put on to a baking tray. Make three other bastilla in the same way and bake for 45 minutes in the centre of a hot oven until crisp and brown. Lower heat if necessary.

Couscous   Morocco

4–6 servings

1 oz chick peas, soaked
   overnight
1 lb mutton
Pinch pepper
1 level teaspoon saffron
12 oz each diced carrots,
   turnip, onions
Little olive oil
2 oz butter
$1\frac{1}{2}$ pints water

Pinch salt
2 tomatoes, skinned
2 oz seedless raisins
Small piece cabbage,
   shredded
$\frac{1}{4}$ lb couscous or Italian
   risotto rice
Cayenne pepper
Paprika

Couscous is a type of semolina made from wheat and can only be obtained in a few specialist shops selling Moroccan and Arabic foods, so use risotto rice as an alternative.

Cook the peas until tender. Cut the meat into neat pieces and toss lightly in the pepper and saffron. Put the chick peas, meat and vegetables into a pan with the oil, half the butter, the water and salt. Simmer slowly for 1¼ hours. Add the tomatoes, raisins and cabbage. Cook for a further 15 minutes. Drain and reserve stock. Boil the couscous in salted water until tender, about ½ hour, strain, blend in remaining butter. Pile into the centre of a dish with the meat and vegetable mixture round.

To make the sauce, which is served separately, blend a little cayenne pepper and paprika with the reserved stock.

Chopped Liver   Israel

1 onion, finely chopped	4 oz chicken liver
1 oz chicken fat	2 hard-boiled eggs, chopped

Fry the onion in chicken fat, then add liver and fry for a few minutes. Blend with the eggs. Serve with bread or toast.

Salads and Vegetables

Aubergines, peppers (both red and green), carrots, green beans, cabbage and lettuce are popular. Tomatoes are large – rather uneven in shape but good in flavour. Marrow is often diced and cooked in a savoury mixture of fried garlic, onion, tomatoes and very little water for the maximum flavour.

Delicious salads are often found in Algeria or Tunisia, and the following is an excellent start to a meal.

Munkaczina   Algeria/Tunisia

2 oranges, peeled and thinly   2 oz stoned olives, chopped
  sliced   Salt and pepper
2 onions, peeled and thinly   1–2 tablespoons salad oil
  sliced

*Mix together oranges, onions and olives. Season to taste and toss
in oil.*

Green Beans with Olive Oil   Turkey

Leytinyagli Fasulya

4 servings

1 lb French or cut green   1 small onion, chopped
  beans, fresh, frozen or   1 green pepper, chopped
  canned   (optional)
5 tablespoons olive oil   Salt and pepper
2 tomatoes or 1 tablespoon   1 teaspoon sugar
  tomato paste

*Allow frozen beans to defrost or drain canned beans. Put the
beans in a saucepan with the olive oil, tomatoes or tomato paste,
onion, green pepper, salt and pepper and sugar. (Fresh beans
require addition of $\frac{3}{4}$ pint water, frozen beans need about $\frac{1}{4}$ pint
water.) Cover and cook until tender and all liquid is absorbed.
Serve cold.*

Fish Dishes

Octopus is plentiful in most of these countries. Squid is also a local fish much used in Greek dishes.

Octopus needs to be thoroughly cleaned and beaten to make it tender. You can often see fishermen doing this on the rocks. Cook the octopus in a pan until it turns red – the ink bag should be discarded before cooking. Cut neatly and skin if wished, and serve in a number of ways. Simmer for a while, if desired, in seasoned water or wine, then dry thoroughly.

To Fry
Coat in thin batter and cook in hot oil until crisp and brown. Serve with lemon wedges.

Octopus or Squid with Onions and Tomatoes
Greece

Cut octopus into neat pieces. Fry sliced onions, crushed garlic and tomatoes in oil, then add the octopus or squid, seasoning, a little white or red wine, and simmer for several hours until really tender.

Fish Stuffed with Dates   North Africa

4 servings

1 whole haddock or codling
   or 4 whiting (about 2 lb)
2 oz rice
1 teaspoon sugar
2 oz almonds, blanched
Powdered ginger
Pinch powdered cinnamon

3 oz butter
Salt and pepper
8–12 oz dessert dates,
   stoned or soaked prunes
¼ pint water
1 onion, finely chopped

Ask your fishmonger to split the fish and remove the backbone. Cook the rice in boiling salted water until just tender, about 12 minutes, then strain. Mix together the cooked rice, sugar, almonds, pinch each of ginger and cinnamon, the butter, and salt and pepper to taste. Stuff the fish with this mixture adding extra salt and pepper to taste together with a layer of dates or prunes. Skewer or tie firmly.

Put into a buttered dish, with the water, another pinch of ginger and the onion. Cook for about 25–30 minutes for small fish, 45 minutes for a large fish, in the centre of a moderate oven until the fish is golden and the liquid almost evaporated.

Pilaff

Pilau

6 servings

3 oz chicken fat
10–12 chicken livers
8 oz carrots, grated
2 onions, chopped
Small bunch parsley,
   chopped
10 oz long-grain rice

$1\frac{3}{4}$ pints chicken stock
   or water
$1\frac{1}{2}$ teaspoons turmeric
Salt and pepper
1 clove garlic, crushed
   (optional)
2 large tomatoes, skinned
   and chopped

Heat the chicken fat in a saucepan, then add the chicken livers and fry lightly. Remove and cut into neat pieces. (They keep moister if treated this way, rather than being diced before frying.) Add the carrots, onions and parsley to the chicken fat remaining in the pan and fry for 5 minutes, taking care the onion does not brown. Add the rest of the ingredients, except tomatoes, but including the liver. Cover the pan tightly and cook without stirring over a low heat for approximately 30 minutes until the rice has absorbed the liquid – it should not become too dry. Finally, add the tomatoes to the rice mixture.

Serve hot as a light lunch dish.

Mutton Pilau Turkey

4 servings

1½ lb mutton, diced
6 oz rice
Salt and pepper
2 oz fat
3 onions, sliced
3 tomatoes, sliced

2 oz pine kernels
2 cloves garlic, crushed
  (optional)
½ teaspoon saffron
Pinch cumin
Pinch coriander

Cover the meat with cold water, bring to the boil and cook for a few minutes. Skim, add the rice, salt and pepper to taste and simmer for 1½ hours.

Heat the fat and fry the onions and tomatoes. Add the pine kernels, onions and tomatoes to the meat. Garlic can be added, if wished, together with the saffron, cumin and coriander.

Harira North Africa/Morocco

4–6 servings

1 oz dried peas
2½ pints water
4 oz beef or mutton, diced
Giblets of 1 chicken
1 onion, chopped
Salt and pepper
Pinch ginger

Pinch saffron
Little chopped parsley
1 oz rice
2 tomatoes, skinned and
  chopped
1 oz butter

108

Soak the peas overnight in 2 pints of the water. Next day, simmer with the meat, giblets, chopped onion, salt and pepper to taste, spices and parsley for about an hour. Remove the flesh from the giblets and chop finely discarding the bones. Return to the pan with the remaining $\frac{1}{2}$ pint water, rice, tomatoes, butter and a little extra seasoning and cook for a further 20 minutes.

Broiled Meat Balls   Turkey

Sis Köfte

2–3 servings

12 oz lamb, minced twice
2 eggs
Salt and pepper

Juice of 1 large onion (see note at end of recipe)
Olive oil

Put the lamb into a bowl, add the eggs, seasoning to taste and onion juice. Mix thoroughly.

Sprinkle olive oil on your hands, take a piece of lamb mixture and form into a firm paste. Press around skewers to make meat balls. Grill steadily, turning to cook on all sides or cook on a turning spit.

To make onion juice: grate the onion, add salt to taste. Allow to stand for 15 minutes, then squeeze through clean muslin or push through a fine sieve.

Cholent Israel

3-lb joint of beef or lamb
4 oz haricot beans, soaked
   overnight
3 oz barley
6 oz small onions
8 oz baby carrots

Salt and pepper
Water
1 lb potatoes, sliced
2 oz kosher margarine
4 oz self-raising flour

Put the beef or lamb into a deep dish with the haricot beans, barley, onions and carrots, season well and cover with water. Cover with a layer of potatoes and add more water to cover them.
   Make the dumplings by mixing together the margarine and flour and adding enough water to give a firm dough. Add to the pan, cover and cook in the centre of a cool oven for several hours.

Kebab with Yoghourt Turkey

2–3 servings

3 loaves of flat bread (also
   called *pide* or holy bread)
8 oz beef or mutton, cut
   into 1-inch cubes
1 tablespoon olive oil
Salt

Onion water (see note at
   end of recipe)
3–4 tomatoes, skinned
1 pint yoghourt
2 oz melted butter

Flat bread can be obtained from Greek and Cypriot shops.
   Cut bread in 1-inch lengths and warm in a cool oven or on a greased griddle. Mix the meat with the olive oil, onion water and salt. Fry this mixture for 5–10 minutes. While the mixture is cooking, cut the tomatoes into pieces and cook to a purée, removing the skins when cooked.

Pour the tomato purée on to the bread lengths, cover with the yoghourt. Add the next layer, this time the fried meat. Top with the melted butter. Serve immediately.

To make onion water: boil sliced onion in a little water until the onion is tender. Strain and use the onion water as required. NB. The butter swims to the surface.

Shish-kebab   Greece

4 servings

1 lb lamb, cut in 1-inch
    cubes
Chopped herbs
Cumin
Caraway
Saffron
Salt and pepper
Oil or melted butter
Small tomatoes (optional)

Small onions, partially
    cooked (optional)
Green or red peppers,
    deseeded and sliced
    (optional)
Aubergines, sliced
    (optional)
8 mushrooms (optional)

Sprinkle the meat generously with the herbs, spices and salt and pepper. Put on to long metal skewers and brush with the oil or melted butter. Cook over a charcoal fire, on a turning-spit or under a grill, until tender. If liked, a selection of the vegetables can be threaded alternately on the skewers with the meat. But quite often the meat is served on its own on a bed of rice.

Meat Casserole with Aubergines

Greece

Moussaka

4–6 servings

4 oz butter
8 oz onions, sliced
2 large aubergines, sliced
1–1½ lb potatoes, peeled
   and sliced
1 oz flour
½ pint milk
Salt and pepper

2–3 oz cheese, grated
1 egg, beaten
1 lb minced meat,
   (preferably raw mutton)
   well seasoned
2–4 tomatoes, sliced
Parsley

*Heat 3 oz butter and fry the onions until tender but not broken.
Remove onions from butter, then fry aubergines and potatoes,
turning until well coated.*

*Make the sauce: heat the remaining 1 oz butter, add the
flour and cook for several minutes, remove from the heat, then
gradually add the milk. Bring slowly to the boil and cook until
thickened and smooth, add salt and pepper and the grated cheese
and beaten egg, stir well but do not cook again.*

*Arrange a layer of the sliced aubergine and potato in a dish,
top with the well-seasoned meat, onion and tomatoes. Put a small
amount of sauce on each layer and continue filling the dish
ending with a layer of potato and aubergine. Cover and bake in a
moderate oven for about 1 hour. Garnish with parsley.*

Almond Pastries   Cyprus

Loukkoumiah

24–30 servings

1 lb fine semolina
6 oz butter
Warm water
8 oz ground almonds
4 oz chopped almonds
4 oz sugar

Orange-flower water or
  grated rind and juice of
  1 orange
4 oz icing sugar
2 oz chopped almonds or
  candied orange peel

These are eaten at wedding parties.

Stir semolina into melted butter, mix well. Leave overnight. Next day, stir in enough warm water to make a pliable dough. Break off small pieces and press or roll into oval or round shapes, enough to hold about 1 tablespoon of filling. Mix ground and chopped almonds and sugar, mix to a paste with orange-flower water or orange rind and juice. Fill pastry shapes, moistening edges and pinching together. Bake in moderately hot oven for about 15 minutes.

When cold, top with soft, orange-flavoured icing made from the icing sugar mixed with orange-flower water. Sprinkle on chopped almonds or candied orange peel.

Börek Pastry   Turkey

1 lb flour
¾ teaspoon salt

4 eggs
Water

Sieve flour and salt, gradually add eggs and water and let the dough stand. Knead and roll out thinly – in Turkey a rolling pin of broomstick size is often used. When pastry is really thin use as follows:

Cheese Börek   Turkey

Peynirli Börek

12–16 servings

Börek pastry (see recipe   Little chopped parsley or
   above)   dill
2 oz suet   I egg yolk, beaten
4–6 oz butter
8 oz cottage cheese or
   other soft white cheese

Cut pastry into squares or ovals. Melt suet and strain, then mix with melted butter and allow to cool. Beat until it is white. Mix cheese with herb of choice. Spread börek pastry shapes with suet and butter mixture and fill centres with the cheese mixture. Turn the edges over to cover filling. Brush top with beaten egg yolk and bake in the centre of a hot oven for about 25–30 minutes.

Cheese Pancakes   Israel

Blintzes

4 servings

4 oz plain flour	3 tablespoons caster sugar
Pinch salt	Few drops vanilla essence
2 eggs	Butter for frying
$\frac{1}{4}$ pint milk	Strawberry jam or
Oil or fat for frying	redcurrant jelly
8 oz cottage cheese	

*Sieve flour and salt, beat to a thick creamy batter with the
eggs and milk. Brush a thick frying-pan with oil or fat, heat, fry
the pancakes until golden brown on both sides. Keep hot.*

*Mix the cottage cheese with the sugar and vanilla essence,
and fill the pancakes with this.*

*Fold as an envelope, heat in hot butter. Serve topped with
hot or cold jam or jelly.*

Chanukah Plum Cake   Israel

10 servings

6 oz butter	8 oz sultanas
6 oz demerara sugar	2 oz sweet almonds,
3 eggs	chopped
8 oz flour	$\frac{1}{2}$ teaspoon mixed spice
1 tablespoon golden syrup	$2\frac{1}{2}$ tablespoons milk
4 oz candied peel	$\frac{1}{4}$ teaspoon bicarbonate of
8 oz currants	soda

Beat the butter and sugar together to a cream. Add each egg separately and beat well. Sift in the flour, add the syrup and stir well, adding fruit, almonds and spice. Heat the milk and dissolve the bicarbonate of soda in it. Stir into the mixture, then turn into a lined 8-inch cake tin and bake for 3 hours in a very slow oven.

When cold the cake may be iced.

Syrup-soaked Cake   Greece/Turkey

Halvas Tis Rinas

8–10 servings

6 oz butter
6 oz sugar
Grated rind and juice of
  lemon or orange or
  1 teaspoon cinnamon or
  $\frac{1}{2}$ teaspoon almond
  essence
3 eggs
9 oz semolina

2 level teaspoons baking
  powder
4 oz chopped almonds
3 tablespoons milk, fruit
  juice or brandy
$\frac{1}{2}$ pint boiling water
4 oz sugar or honey
Juice of 1 lemon or orange

Cream the butter with the sugar, then add grated citrus rind, or cinnamon or almond essence to flavour. Gradually beat in the eggs, add the semolina and baking powder, chopped almonds and bind with the milk, fruit juice or brandy. Put into a well-greased 9-inch tin and bake for about 50 minutes in the centre of a moderate oven. Meanwhile, mix the boiling water with the sugar or honey and citrus juice and when the cake is turned out, pour over the syrup.

Turkish Delight   Turkey

1 lb loaf sugar
½ pint water
1 oz gelatine
2 tablespoons lemon juice
Rose-water

Few drops cochineal
Few drops vanilla essence
Sieved icing sugar
Cornflour

Put sugar and water into a saucepan, heat slowly and stir until the sugar has dissolved. Add the gelatine blended with the lemon juice. Simmer gently for about 10 minutes. Remove from the heat. Pour half into a basin and add a little rose-water and a few drops cochineal to this and stir.

Pour into an oiled tin and allow to set. Stir in a few drops of vanilla essence to the mixture remaining in the saucepan. Keep this in a warm place so that it does not set. When the pink layer is firm, pour the cold white layer on top. Cut into squares with a hot knife. Roll in sieved icing sugar and a little cornflour.

Turkish Coffee   Turkey

Turkish coffee is made in a special copper pot with a long handle, called an *ibrik*, but if not available use a small saucepan.

For each portion, use 1 coffee cup of water, 1 teaspoon sugar, 3–4 teaspoons pulverized coffee (obtainable in specialist coffee shops).

Bring the water to the boil, add the sugar and coffee, stir well. Boil 3 times. Remove from the heat, add a few drops of cold water. Remove the froth from the surface of the coffee, divide between the cups, pour the rest of the coffee slowly into the cups.

Scandinavia

Scandinavia

Scandinavian food is both interesting and colourful for the cooks of these countries have established a very high standard of presentation and garnish.

Fish is particularly good in Norway; open sandwiches in Denmark. The most attractive salads and ways of serving herrings are from Sweden.

Dishes in Finland have affinity with those of both Russia and Scandinavia.

Open Sandwiches   Denmark

Smørrebrød

These can be a complete meal or a first course. Butter white, brown or rye bread or crispbread, then top with some of the following:

1. Hard-boiled egg, sliced tomato and crisp bacon.
2. Creamed liver pâté topped with red cabbage and sliced orange.
3. Thick slices of Camembert cheese topped with cherries and parsley.
4. Slices of luncheon meat topped with potato, salami, twists of lemon, cucumber, tomato and watercress.
5. Slices of Samsoe cheese garnished with a radish flower.
6. Curls of salami on soft cream cheese.
7. Prawns on a bed of lettuce, with mayonnaise and twists of lemon.
8. Liver pâté decorated with sliced red pepper and soft creamy mayonnaise and a prune.
9. Potato salad on a bed of lettuce with a cheese-flavoured mayonnaise, pieces of orange and a grape.
10. Rolls of salami or ham garnished with raw onion.
11. Liver pâté or salami garnished with raw mushroom, gherkin and tomato.
12. Danish Blue cheese with a flower made of thin pieces of carrot and a grape.
13. Luncheon meat topped with Russian or potato salad, tomato and cucumber.
14. Smoked eel with scrambled egg.
15. Smoked salmon, prawns and lemon.

Be sure to use plenty of crisp lettuce under the toppings.

White Fish Soup   Norway

Fiskesuppe

8 servings

2 lb cod	$2\frac{1}{2}$ oz flour
1 cod's head	$\frac{1}{2}$ pint milk
2 onions, quartered	1 glass white wine
4 sticks celery, diced	2 tablespoons lemon juice
1 clove garlic, crushed (optional)	4 oz peeled prawns
	Chopped parsley
Salt and pepper	

Put the cod, cod's head, onions, celery and crushed garlic in a pan, season, cover with cold water. Bring to the boil, simmer for 15 minutes until fish is cooked. Remove fish, strain stock and return to pan. Blend the flour with the milk, add the wine and mix well. Add to fish stock and stir until thickened. Flake half of cooked fish and add to the soup, simmer for 4–5 minutes. Add lemon juice, prawns and remaining pieces of fish. Garnish with parsley.

Herring Salad   Sweden

Sillsalad

4 servings

4 large herrings	$\frac{3}{4}$ pint water
$\frac{1}{4}$ pint white vinegar	1 cucumber
4 peppercorns	2 red eating apples
2 bay leaves	$\frac{1}{4}$ pint sour cream*
1 small onion, sliced	Salt and pepper

*You can buy cartons of cultured sour cream, or use yoghourt, or fresh cream plus 1 tablespoon lemon juice.

122

Remove heads, intestines and backbones from the herrings, leaving about ½ inch of bone at the tail end, and wash well. Roll up herrings, starting at the head end. Put herrings into a deep casserole, add the vinegar, peppercorns, bay leaves and onion together with the water. Cover the dish and bake in the centre of a very moderate oven for 30 minutes. Leave to cool in the liquid, then drain. Peel cucumber, and cut into dice. Core and dice apples, leaving skin on. Put into a bowl with the diced cucumber. Add the cream and seasoning to taste. Mix well. Serve cucumber mixture on a long dish, place herring rolls on top.

Mustard Sauce   Denmark

This is delicious with herrings or with pickled salmon – a speciality in Denmark.

2 oz sugar
1 tablespoon vinegar

1 tablespoon French
  mustard
3 tablespoons salad oil
Little chopped dill

Put the sugar and vinegar into a pan, stir for a few minutes over a moderate heat, then add the mustard, salad oil and a little chopped dill.

Salads

Salads form part of the important cold table which is found in Scandinavian countries, together with smoked eel, smoked salmon, herrings treated in various ways, shellfish, and a wonderful choice of meats and cheeses.

Klampenborg Salad   Denmark

Klampergsalat

¼ pint mayonnaise
1–2 teaspoons curry
  powder
¼ pint double cream,
  whipped

1½ lb white cabbage,
  shredded
Grapes
Walnuts
Chopped dill

Mix together the mayonnaise, curry powder and cream. Toss the cabbage in this and garnish with grapes, walnuts and dill.

Pickled Fresh Cucumber   Sweden

Inlagd Gurka

1 large cucumber
3 tablespoons vinegar
2 tablespoons water
2 tablespoons sugar

¼ teaspoon salt
Dash white pepper
1 tablespoon parsley,
  chopped

Wipe the cucumber, slice without peeling and put in a dish. Mix together the remaining ingredients. Pour over cucumber. Allow to stand 2–3 hours in refrigerator or cool place before serving. Serve with meat and salads.

Vegetable Dishes

During the cold winters, particularly in the northern part of Scandinavia, the selection of fresh vegetables is limited, but during the summer these are excellent.

124

Red cabbage is used often for cooking instead of green, and caraway seeds are added during the process of cooking.

Burning Love   Denmark

Braendende Karlighted

4 servings

$\frac{1}{4}$ pint milk
3 oz butter
1 lb mashed potatoes
Salt and pepper

2–3 large onions, sliced
4 tomatoes, sliced or
   2 cooked beetroot, diced
8 oz bacon rashers

Mix the milk and 1 oz butter with the hot potatoes and salt and pepper to taste. Beat until white and fluffy. Fry the onions in the rest of the butter until light brown. Heat the tomatoes or beetroot. Fry the bacon rashers until crisp. Pile the hot creamed potatoes on a flat warm dish. Arrange the fried bacon on top, garnish with tomatoes or beetroot and onions. Serve hot.

Sugar Browned Potatoes   Denmark

6–8 servings

These are particularly good with rather rich food like pork.

2 lb new potatoes
1$\frac{1}{2}$ oz sugar

1$\frac{1}{2}$ oz butter

Boil the potatoes in boiling salted water until cooked but still firm. Put the sugar into a frying-pan or large shallow saucepan, stir over a moderate heat until melted, then add the butter. Toss the potatoes very carefully in this mixture until evenly coated. They may sound odd but they do taste delicious.

Fish Balls   Norway

Fiskelbollar

6 servings

2 lb uncooked fish, preferably haddock, filleted	1 oz butter
2 teaspoons salt	Pinch nutmeg
2 tablespoons potato flour or cornflour	Pinch pepper
2 tablespoons flour	Milk
	2–3 tablespoons cream
	Fish stock

Mince fish two or three times until very fine. Beat with the salt for 15 minutes until a soft dough. Add potato flour or cornflour, flour, butter and spices. Add a little boiled milk and cream gradually. Form into tiny balls. Cook these in milk or fish stock for about 15 minutes. The liquid can be thickened for a sauce.

Fish Pudding

Fiskebudding

6 servings

1½–2 lb fish (use trout, haddock or a white fish such as cod), filleted	Salt and pepper
2 oz margarine or butter	1 oz flour
2 eggs	2½ tablespoons milk or top of milk

Put boned uncooked fish through a mincer twice. Melt the margarine or butter, add to fish with the remaining ingredients. Put the mixture into a well-greased basin and cover with greased paper and a cloth or foil. Either steam for 45 minutes or stand the pudding in a dish of cold water in a moderate oven and cook for 30 minutes. Turn out carefully.

To make an even lighter pudding, separate the egg yolks from the whites, add the yolks first, then fold in the stiffly beaten egg whites.

Apple Cake

Aeblekage

1½ lb apples, peeled, cored and sliced	Sugar
4 oz butter	2 oz dried breadcrumbs
	Whipped cream

Cook apple slices gently in half the butter until soft, adding sugar to taste. Mix 2 oz sugar and the breadcrumbs and brown in the remaining butter. Allow to cool in the pan.

Put alternate layers of apple purée and buttered breadcrumbs
in a bowl, making the bottom and top layer breadcrumbs.
Decorate with whipped cream.

Christmas Biscuits   Denmark

8 oz plain flour   Cinnamon
½ teaspoon baking powder   1 oz blanched almonds,
6 oz butter   chopped
4 oz caster sugar   1 oz ground almonds
1 egg, beaten   ½ teaspoon vanilla essence

Sieve together flour and baking powder. Rub in 5 oz butter until
the mixture is like fine breadcrumbs. Stir in 3 oz sugar and add
enough egg to make a soft smooth dough. Divide into three
portions and use for the following.

Finnish bread
Roll out one portion of the dough into a long sausage about 1½
inches in diameter. Flatten top slightly with rolling pin. Cut into
slices ½ inch thick, on a slant. Place on greased baking trays and
bake in a moderately hot oven for about 15 minutes until firm and
a pale honey colour.

Jewish cakes
Roll out the second portion very thinly, cut into 1½-inch rounds.
Mix together the cinnamon, remaining sugar and chopped
blanched almonds. Brush with beaten egg and sprinkle with
cinnamon mixture. Bake as above for 7 minutes until firm.

Vanilla rings
Into the remaining dough beat the remaining butter, the ground
almonds and the vanilla essence. Place in a forcing bag with a
medium-sized star pipe. Pipe into rings, approximately 2 inches

in diameter, on a lightly greased baking sheet. Bake as above for 10 minutes until firm and honey coloured. Leave plain or top with sieved icing sugar.

Fruit Fool   Denmark

Rodgrod

2 kinds of red fruit	Chopped almonds
Sugar to taste	Cream
Cornflour	

Two kinds of fruit, such as raspberries and redcurrants, produce a better flavour than a single fruit. Take equal quantities of each, wash, put into saucepan with water to just cover. Stew gently until very soft. Rub through fine sieve, return juice to saucepan. Add sugar to sweeten, bring mixture to the boil. For each pint of juice use 1 tablespoon cornflour, blended first with a little cold water. Add to fruit juice, boil until clear, stirring constantly. Turn into a dish, decorate with chopped almonds and serve with plenty of cream.

Christmas Rice Pudding   Scandinavia

4–6 servings

Traditionally, 3 oz rice is cooked with milk or milk and water flavoured with a little sugar and cinnamon, and often made extra rich by beating in a little cream. One tradition is to put an almond in the pudding and whoever finds it has a happy year. The following recipe is a delicious cold sweet based on this.

Rice Cream Scandinavia

8–10 servings

3 oz rice
2 pints boiling water
½ teaspoon salt
2 teaspoons powdered
   gelatine
2½ tablespoons sherry

6 tablespoons sugar
4 oz chopped almonds
1 pint double cream or
   evaporated milk
1–2 teaspoons vanilla

Wash rice and drain. Stir slowly into the boiling salted water. Cover and cook without stirring until tender. Drain, rinse with cold water and drain again. Stir gelatine into sherry, put in a basin over hot water to dissolve. Add to rice with sugar and almonds. Cool. Whip the cream, fold in vanilla and mix with the rice. Pour into a wet mould. Chill for several hours. Unmould on to a serving dish and serve with a cold fruit purée.

Spain and
Portugal

Spain and Portugal

To most people Spain is a country of sunshine, sandy beaches and happy holiday memories. The basic peasant Spanish dish of paella (see page 134) has become a tourist treat along with zarzuela (mixed fish – see page 134). Churros (see page 135) you can buy in the street for a few pesetas and Spanish omelettes (see page 135) are a standby to serve hot for a light meal or cold for a packed lunch.

Portugal shares the Atlantic coastline with north-west Spain and therefore fish is plentiful. They also have some very special egg dishes that are very easy to prepare.

For some of these recipes I have given no quantities in the list of ingredients because, as peasant dishes, their charm lies in being able to use what you have to hand, making a little or a lot as you wish. Just the sort of tasty dishes to give unexpected guests!

Hors d'oeuvres Spain and Portugal

It is usual to be offered a delicious selection of bite-sized appetizers with a drink. Tiny portions of fried octopus, shellfish, vegetables coated in batter and fried, olives or salted almonds.

Eggs are often used as more formal hors d'oeuvres, see the omelette on page 135, or the following:

Portuguese Eggs Portugal

Fry tomatoes and onions in a little butter, then put into individual heat-proof dishes. Break an egg on top, and top with crumbs and salt and pepper; bake until set.

The Spanish version of this recipe is more elaborate, in which a vegetable mixture similar to Letscho (see page 56) but flavoured with garlic is made and the eggs cooked on this, then topped with cheese sauce or grated cheese, and set.

Fish Dishes Spain

Shellfish of all kinds as well as good white fish abound. One of the most delicious and colourful of Spanish dishes is zarzuela.

Zarzuela   Spain

*Fry in equal quantities of butter and oil, diced white fish and a
mixture of lobster, shrimps or prawns. When tender, add a little
brandy, then a mixture of fried onions, garlic and tomatoes
(to give a soft purée-like sauce).*

*Season and just cover with wine and lemon juice, if wished,
and heat through. Mussels may be added, if liked.*

Chicken and Fish Rice   Spain

Paella

4–8 servings

1 small chicken	8 oz fresh green beans or
4 oz lean pork, diced	frozen beans or frozen
3 tablespoons olive oil	peas
1 clove garlic, crushed	4 oz rice
2 tomatoes, peeled and	1 pint well-seasoned stock
chopped	$\frac{1}{4}$ teaspoon saffron
	4 oz shelled shrimps
	Few clams or mussels

*Cut the chicken into 8 pieces and fry with the pork in the olive
oil in a large heavy pan. When well browned, add garlic and
tomatoes, cook 1 minute. Add beans or peas, rice, stock and
saffron, bring to the boil, boil 4 minutes uncovered, then lower
heat and cook until the rice is tender. Fry shrimps separately in a
little olive oil, add shrimps and prepared mussels or clams as a
garnish to the rice, just before serving.*

Spanish Omelette

Tortilla

2–3 servings

4–6 eggs	Filling of choice (see below)
Salt and pepper	2 tablespoons olive oil

Beat the eggs with salt and pepper to taste. Add the prepared filling. Cook in the hot oil until lightly set on the bottom side, then finish cooking either in the oven or under the grill with the heat turned low. This type of omelette is always served flat. It tastes equally good hot or cold.

Selection of fillings:
(a) Mixture of fried chopped red and green pepper, onion, tomato and crushed garlic.
(b) Above mixture simmered in stock instead of fried.
(c) Mixed cooked shellfish.
(d) Mixed chopped salami and cooked vegetables.

Fried Choux Pastry

Spain

Churros

Ingredients as choux pastry, see page 79

Oil for deep frying
Icing sugar, sieved

Make the choux pastry and put into a piping bag with a plain nozzle. This should be no wider than ½ inch.

Heat the oil. Squeeze the piping bag with the left hand and cut off into 12-inch sticks with a pair of scissors in the right hand.

Drop into and fry in the hot oil until crisp and golden brown. Drain and sprinkle with sieved icing sugar. Serve hot or cold.

Egg Pudding

Pudim de ovas

6 servings

10 oz sugar	Rind and juice of 1 lemon
2 tablespoons water	8 egg yolks, beaten
Knob butter	

Boil 2 oz sugar with 2 tablespoons water until a golden caramel – coat a mould or basin with this. Boil 8 oz sugar, small knob butter and rind and juice of the lemon until syrupy, cool, then strain over the beaten egg yolks. Put into caramel-lined mould, cover with foil or greased greaseproof paper. Steam for about 45 minutes over hot but not boiling water. Turn out when cool.

Portuguese Pudding

Portugal

Pudim Portugaise

6 servings

12 oz sugar	6 egg yolks
Juice of 6 large oranges	

Put the sugar into a heavy pan with the orange juice. Stir well to dissolve sugar, then boil until it becomes a thickish syrup. Remove from heat, cool slightly, then whisk in the egg yolks.

Transfer to a well-greased mould and cover with greased greaseproof paper or foil. Steam for about 45 minutes over hot but not boiling water. Turn out when cool.

China, Japan and Far East

China

Chinese cooking has always been popular. All their dishes are prepared with great care and give a blend of interesting flavours, the combination of sweet and sour tastes being particularly subtle. Soups on the whole are light so that they do not spoil the appetite for further dishes. Pork is a favourite meat. Among favourite Chinese vegetables are bean sprouts, bamboo shoots and mushrooms. Most of these can be obtained from stores specializing in Chinese and Oriental food.

Japan

Japanese food relies on the freshness of the ingredients, the best known, internationally, being Tempura and Sukiyaki. Tea, served without milk or sugar is the national drink. Saké is the famous rice wine of Japan – dry sherry can be substituted where necessary.

Meatball Soup　　　　　　　　　　China

4 servings

4–6 oz lean pork, minced
1 tablespoon soya sauce
1 tablespoon sherry
2 teaspoons spring onion,
　finely chopped

2 teaspoons finely chopped
　preserved ginger
1 teaspoon cornflour
Salt and pepper
1½ pints good chicken or
　beef stock

Mix the pork with the soya sauce, sherry, onion, ginger, corn-
flour and season to taste. Form into tiny balls each one about the
size of a hazelnut. Heat the stock and poach the balls in this for
about 5 minutes, then serve.

To make a more interesting soup, you can heat bean sprouts or
finely shredded bamboo shoots in the stock before adding the
meatballs.

Bean Sprout Soup　　　　　　　　Korea

Kong Na-mool Kook

4–6 servings

4 spring onions, chopped
1 clove garlic, chopped
3–4 oz fillet steak, diced
Salt and pepper

2 tablespoons soya sauce
12 oz fresh or canned bean
　shoots
1½ pints chicken stock

Put the spring onions, garlic and beef into the pan with the salt
and pepper, soya sauce, fresh bean shoots and stock. Simmer

*gently until the meat is tender — about 15 minutes. If using
canned bean shoots, add after 5 minutes' cooking.*

Rice and Potatoes   Far East

Kahm-cha-pahb

4 servings

1 cup long-grain rice	2 cups water
1 cup uncooked sweet potatoes or yam, peeled and diced	Salt and pepper

*Put the rice and potatoes, or yam, into a pan. Add the water
and season to taste. Cook for 20 minutes without stirring.
This is often served as a first course.*

Plain Fried Rice   Far East

4–6 servings

1 lb long-grain rice	Oil

*Partially cook the rice in boiling salted water until nearly
tender. Do not over cook. Drain well. Fry in the hot oil until very
crisp.*

Plain Fried Noodles   Far East

4–6 servings

1 lb noodles   Oil

Cook the noodles in boiling salted water until nearly tender. Rinse in cold water and dry thoroughly. Fry in the hot oil until very crisp.

Special Fried Rice   China

Gai Dan Chow Fan

3–4 servings

12 oz cooked rice
3 tablespoons oil
1 onion, finely chopped
4 oz cooked shrimps, diced
  ham or chicken

3 oz bamboo shoots,
  shredded
1 tablespoon soya sauce
Salt and pepper
3 eggs, beaten

Break the grains of rice apart with a fork, so they will heat quickly. Heat the oil in a pan, then add the onion, shrimps or meat, shredded bamboo shoots, soya sauce and rice and heat thoroughly, stirring. Add the well-seasoned beaten eggs and continue cooking until the eggs are just set. Serve at once.

Curried Fried Rice

China

Chia Li Chao Fan

4 servings

12 oz cooked rice
1 small onion, finely
  chopped
3 tablespoons oil
½–1 tablespoon curry
  powder
6 oz cooked lean pork,
  shredded

3 oz cooked chicken,
  shredded
2 oz bean shoots
2 oz water chestnuts
1 oz blanched almonds
1 tablespoon soya sauce

Fork the rice to separate the grains. Fry the onion in the hot oil, add the curry powder and the rest of the ingredients and heat together, stirring all the time. Serve by itself, or as part of a Chinese meal with Omelette (see page 146) and Chop Suey (see page 151).

Tea Eggs

Japan

4 servings

4 hard-boiled eggs
Pot of strong China tea
Salt and pepper

Soya sauce
Anise

Crack the eggs leaving the shells on, put in a pan and add the tea (including the tea leaves), seasoning to taste, a little soya sauce and a few drops of anise. Simmer for an hour, making sure the pan doesn't boil dry. These are excellent for picnics.

Egg Rolls

2 servings

3 eggs, beaten
Salt and pepper
Oil
Cooked chicken or pork,
  diced

Soya sauce
Small onion, finely chopped
1 teaspoon chopped ginger
Batter (see Fried Prawns,
  page 147)

Season the eggs with salt and pepper. Cook in a little oil to make a firm omelette. Blend the meat with a little soya sauce, the onion and ginger. Spread over the omelette as for a pancake. Roll up and dip in the very thin batter and fry in hot oil for a few minutes.

Fragrant Aubergine

Chiehtze Hsiang

4–6 servings

2 aubergines or egg plants
3 teaspoons cornflour
Salt and pepper
Oil for deep frying
3 oz cooked chicken,
  shredded
4 oz cooked ham, shredded
2 oz almonds or walnuts,
  shredded

4 prepared Chinese
  mushrooms (see page 151)
  or 8 fresh mushrooms,
  chopped
2 tablespoons chicken stock
1–2 tablespoons soy sauce
1 tablespoon sherry
1 teaspoon sugar

143

Wipe the aubergines and cut into thin slices. Mix the cornflour with seasoning, dust the aubergine slices sparingly with this and fry in hot, deep oil until crisp and golden brown. Drain on absorbent paper and put on to a hot dish to keep warm.

To make the sauce heat I tablespoon oil then add the chicken, ham, nuts and mushrooms. Add the remaining ingredients and heat through.

Pour the hot sauce over the aubergine slices and serve.

Fried Dumplings   China

Kuo Tich Chiao Tzu

4–6 servings

12 oz flour	Oil for deep frying
Pinch salt	4 tablespoons chicken stock
Water to bind	(optional)
Use the filling for Chinese	
Ravioli (see page 150)	

Mix the flour, salt and enough water to make a soft, yet pliable dough. Take off tiny pieces the size of a small walnut and make a hole in the centre of each for the filling or if preferred press out into a flat pancake shape. Insert the filling into the hole or put on the flat cake and roll with your floured hands into a round dumpling so that the filling is covered with the dough. Fry in hot oil for about 8 minutes until very crisp and golden brown. Drain on absorbent paper and serve immediately.

If preferred, fry in 2–3 tablespoons hot oil in a pan, turning over until golden on the outside. Pour over about 4 tablespoons boiling seasoned chicken stock. Cover the pan, lower the heat so the dumplings will not burn and cook for about 12 minutes.

144

Fish   Japan

The Japanese have a superabundance of good fresh fish and
there are many dishes similar to the following with local
variations. The amounts vary according to the importance
of the dish in the meal and the number of people served.

Fish Salad   Japan

Lettuce, finely shredded   Soy sauce
White fish and shellfish,
  diced

*Arrange the lettuce on a serving dish. Decorate it with neat
little heaps of fish and shellfish and sprinkle soy sauce over it.
The fish must be very fresh.*

Salted Fish   Japan

6 servings

Salted fish is delicious with rice.

1 lb white fish or mackerel,   Salt and pepper, generous
  cleaned, boned and diced   amount to taste
2 tablespoons soy sauce   1 spring onion, chopped
2 tablespoons water   1 clove garlic, crushed
1 tablespoon sugar   Little chopped ginger
                                    (optional)

*Blend the fish with the rest of the ingredients. Simmer gently
for a few minutes until the fish is tender. Serve immediately.*

Crab Omelette China

Foo Yung Hai

2 servings

2–3 oz crabmeat, flaked
2 tablespoons chicken stock
2 teaspoons soy sauce
2 teaspoons spring onion,
  finely chopped

2 tablespoons bean shoots
3–4 eggs
Salt and pepper
2 tablespoons oil

*Mix the crabmeat, stock, soy sauce, onion, bean shoots, eggs
and seasoning together. Heat the oil in the pan, pour in the
omelette mixture and allow to cook steadily until just set. Either
serve flat as a Spanish omelette or cut into strips and serve with a
savoury dish such as Chop Suey (see page 151).*

Chinese Savoury Omelette China

2–3 servings

1 dried mushroom (see
  note on page 151) soaked
  and sliced or 2–3 fresh
  mushrooms, sliced
1 oz cooked ham, sliced
1–2 shelled shrimps or
  prawns, chopped
1 tablespoon bamboo
  shoots, finely chopped

1 tablespoon water
  chestnut, finely chopped
1 tablespoon bean shoots
1 tablespoon cornflour
2 tablespoons water
Salt and pepper
Few drops dry sherry
4 eggs, beaten
2 tablespoons oil for frying

Mix the mushroom, ham, shrimps or prawns and the vegetables together. Blend the cornflour with the water, seasoning and sherry, add to the vegetable mixture. Lastly, add the well-beaten eggs. Heat the oil in a 7-inch omelette pan, then pour in the egg mixture and cook steadily until quite set. Cut into narrow strips and serve over Fried Rice (see page 141) or on top of a savoury dish such as Fragrant Aubergine (see page 143).

The omelette will serve several more people if used as a garnish.

Fried Prawns   Far East

4 servings

To prepare 1 lb large prawns, make a batter of 1 tablespoon cornflour, 3 egg whites, seasoning, little chopped onion (or use 1 egg white and 3 tablespoons water instead of all egg whites). Coat the prawns and fry in hot oil for a few minutes.

The dish can be varied by adding a little soy sauce or sherry to the batter.

In Korea, egg yolks are added to the batter.

The Japanese method is to coat the prawns with rice flour instead of cornflour, and serve the prawns on a bed of fried green peppers.

Vegetable Fritters   Japan

Tempura I

Tempura is a delicious Japanese fried food. Although the following recipe is for vegetables, a similar one can be used for prawns or shrimps.

Vegetables used are cucumber, carrots, daikon (Japanese radish) or small pieces of turnip. The Japanese also use a green vegetable as well.

4 oz flour	Vegetable of choice
1 egg	Oil for deep frying
$\frac{1}{4}$ pint water	

Make a batter by blending first three ingredients together. Dip vegetables into this, fry in hot oil.

Tempura II

Soy sauce	Batter (see page 147)
Vinegar	Oil for deep frying
Fish or shellfish, cut into	
bite-sized pieces or	
pressed into little balls	

Make a marinade with the soy sauce and vinegar. Marinade the fish in this for about 2 hours, turning the fish from time to time. Dip the fish in the batter and deep fry until golden brown. Serve immediately.

Eggs and Tomatoes   Japan

3 eggs	3 tomatoes, skinned and
Soy sauce	chopped
Oil	

Beat the eggs with the soy sauce to taste. Heat a little oil in a pan and pour in the egg mixture to make an omelette. When the egg begins to set, add the tomatoes and continue cooking until the egg mixture is firm.

Fish in Hot Sauce   China

Kan Shao Yu

4 servings

1¼–1½ lb whole white fish
Salt and pepper
Oil for deep frying
1 oz lard or 1 tablespoon
  oil
1–2 cloves garlic, finely
  chopped
2 tablespoons preserved
  ginger, sliced
2 small spring onions,
  sliced

2 red chillis, chopped
  (optional) or 2 table-
  spoons sliced bamboo
  shoots
2 tablespoons Chinese rice
  wine or sherry
1½ tablespoons soy sauce
Few drops chilli sauce
2 tablespoons sugar

Split the fish and clean it well, but leave the head and tail on. Season well with salt and pepper. Make several slits in the fish so that the flesh can absorb the sauce. Fry the fish in the hot oil until just tender, but unbroken. Meanwhile, make the sauce: heat the lard or oil, fry the garlic in it, then add the ginger, spring onions and chillis or bamboo shoots and the remaining ingredients with salt and pepper to taste. Heat for about 3 minutes. When the fish is cooked, remove from oil on to a hot dish, then pour over the very hot sauce.

Note: For chillis, substitute sliced bamboo shoots if you don't like a hot flavoured sauce.

Chinese Ravioli China

4–5 servings

8 oz flour
Pinch salt
2 eggs plus 1 egg white
1 tablespoon oil
8 oz minced raw pork or
  chicken
2 spring onions, finely
  chopped
2 teaspoons finely chopped
  preserved ginger

1 tablespoon chopped
  blanched almonds
Salt and pepper
Few drops soy sauce
Few drops dry sherry
2 mushrooms, sliced
Little cornflour
¼ pint chicken stock

*Sieve the flour and salt, add the 2 eggs and knead well. If neces-
sary, add a few drops of water to give a firm rolling pasta
dough.*

*To make the filling, heat the oil and toss the meat in it for a few
minutes, then add the rest of the ingredients, except cornflour,
egg white and stock. Roll out the dough into a paper-thin layer
using cornflour on the pastry board, and cut in half. Mark one
layer into about 25–30 small squares and put filling in the centre
of each. Brush the edges of the squares with the egg white, then
cover with the remaining dough, press down well round the
filling, and cut into squares, sealing the edges very firmly.
If possible, leave the dough for 1 hour so that it becomes firm.*

*Put into a pan of boiling salted water and boil for about 15
minutes. Drain and serve with a little very well-seasoned heated
chicken stock.*

Chicken Chop Suey

Chop Suey Gai

4 servings

1 oz dried mushrooms, soaked (see below)
6 oz bean sprouts
6 oz bamboo shoots
2–3 spring onions or 1 leek
3 skinned tomatoes
12 oz cooked chicken
2 tablespoons oil
2 teaspoons cornflour
Salt and pepper

3 tablespoons chicken stock
1 tablespoon soy sauce
1 tablespoon dry sherry
2 tablespoons canned pineapple, drained and chopped
2 tablespoons pineapple syrup (from canned pineapple)

As most people appreciate, chop suey is not a classic Chinese dish – the name simply means a pleasant mixture of ingredients – but it has become a well-known Anglo-Chinese dish.

To make this particular version of the dish cut the mushrooms into thin strips, then chop the vegetables except the bean sprouts into small pieces and cut the chicken into narrow strips. Toss in the hot oil until very hot, do not over-cook.

Meanwhile, blend the cornflour with the rest of the ingredients, add to the chicken mixture, and heat steadily, stirring well, until it thickens and becomes clear. Serve with fried rice (see page 140) or fried noodles (see page 141) and more soy sauce.

Note: Chinese dried mushrooms are quite different from fresh mushrooms; they can be obtained from stores selling Oriental foods. Soak in cold water for several hours, drain, discard stalks, then slice. Instead of 1 oz dried mushrooms use 2–3 oz fresh.

Fried Chicken with Green Pepper China

Gong Ho Gai Deng

4 servings

2 oz blanched almonds
4 tablespoons corn oil
Uncooked breast of 2 young
  chickens, cut into strips
2 teaspoons cornflour
Salt and pepper
1 green pepper, deseeded
  and sliced
1 bamboo shoot, sliced

2 oz water chestnuts,
  sliced
2 spring onions, sliced
2 tablespoons chicken stock
1–1½ tablespoons soy sauce
1 tablespoon sliced
  preserved ginger
½ tablespoon ginger syrup
1 tablespoon dry sherry

Dry the blanched almonds thoroughly and fry in half the oil until golden brown. Remove nuts from the pan, reserving the oil. Coat the chicken in the cornflour and seasoning. Toss the vegetables in the reserved oil in the pan for a few minutes. Remove when slightly browned and mix with the almonds. Wipe out the frying pan if it is at all sticky, before cooking the chicken. Put the remaining oil in the frying pan. Fry the chicken pieces until pale golden brown and tender. Add the chicken stock, soy sauce, ginger, ginger syrup and sherry to the pan and heat through. Stir in the vegetables and nuts and heat thoroughly. Serve with fried rice (see page 140) or fried noodles (see page 141).

Garlic Spare Ribs   China

Kao Pai Ku

4 servings

1½–2 lb spare ribs of pork   Pinch chilli powder
2–3 cloves garlic, crushed   (optional)
Small piece ginger root or   2–3 tablespoons soy sauce
    preserved ginger, crushed   Salt and pepper
1 tablespoon sherry or   2 teaspoons sugar
    brandy

*Separate the spare ribs and put into a roasting tin. Mix the
rest of the ingredients and pour over the spare ribs and leave
for at least an hour. Turn the meat round once or twice in the
marinade until thinly but evenly coated. Cook the meat for
about 1 hour in a moderately hot oven until very crisp and
brown. Serve as the first course of a Chinese meal or for an
unusual barbecue dish.*

Fried Rice and Pork   Indonesia

Nasi Goreng

6 servings

This has been popular in Holland ever since the Dutch
governed the Dutch East Indies.

2 medium onions, sliced   2 tablespoons soy sauce
4 oz butter   Salt and pepper
12 oz diced pork   2 eggs
8 oz cooked rice, rinsed   1 tablespoon water
12 oz vegetables, diced and   Tomatoes, sliced
    cooked   Lettuce
1–2 teaspoons curry powder

Fry the onions in half the butter, then add the pork and cook for 20 minutes, turning from time to time. Add the remaining butter, the rice, vegetables, curry powder, soy sauce and seasoning. Heat through. Make an omelette with the eggs, water and salt and pepper to taste. Pile pork mixture on a hot dish and top with the omelette cut into narrow strips. Serve with a salad of tomatoes and lettuce.

In Holland, this dish is also served with Kroepoek – prawn flavoured crisps – which are bought in packets and fried in hot fat.

Sukiyaki   Japan

2–3 servings

Sukiyaki is cooked at the table. In Japan a spirit lamp and a special saucepan are used. If you want to try a really authentic Sukiyaki, a chafing dish would work quite well, or even an electric frying-pan.

3 tablespoons stock
2–6 tablespoons soy sauce
2 tablespoons sugar
$\frac{1}{2}$ tablespoon saké or sherry
1 tablespoon olive oil or corn oil
8 oz fillet steak, or topside or sirloin cut in thin strips
1 onion, sliced
1 leek, sliced
4 oz cabbage, shredded
2–4 oz mushrooms, finely sliced
4 oz spinach, finely chopped
2 eggs
Salt and pepper
1–2 tablespoons sugar
4 oz cooked rice

Mix together stock, soy sauce, sugar and saké or sherry. (Add soy sauce gradually, tasting frequently as it is quite strong, and you may want to limit the amount you use.) Heat oil in large

154

frying-pan, brown meat on both sides. Add half the sauce to the meat. Push meat to one side of the pan, add onion, leek and cabbage, cook gently for 3 minutes. Add remaining sauce, the mushrooms and spinach. Cook for a further 3 minutes. Beat eggs and season with salt, pepper and sugar. Heat in a separate large pan stirring until slightly thickened but not set. Add hot meat and vegetables to this.

Serve with cooked rice.

Sweet and Sour Pork   China

Go Lo Yuk

3–4 servings

3 oz flour
$\frac{1}{2}$ teaspoon baking powder
$\frac{1}{2}$ small egg, beaten
$\frac{1}{4}$ pint water
$\frac{1}{2}$ teaspoon oil
1 tablespoon pickled
  cabbage
1 tablespoon cucumber
1 tablespoon carrots
1 tablespoon salt
1 tablespoon vinegar
6–8 oz leg of pork

Salt and pepper
$\frac{1}{2}$ teaspoon oil
$\frac{1}{2}$ teaspoon sherry
1 tablespoon flour
Oil for deep frying
$\frac{3}{4}$ teaspoon cornflour
2 teaspoons sugar
$\frac{1}{2}$ teaspoon soy sauce
$\frac{1}{4}$ pint water or pineapple
  syrup
Monosodium glutamate

To prepare the batter, sieve the flour and baking powder, add the egg, water and oil.

Prepare vegetables by cutting 1 tablespoon each of pickled cabbage, cucumber and carrot, if liked, into matchsticks, sprinkle with the salt. Allow to stand for 5 minutes, press out liquid, then add the vinegar. Cut the pork into 1-inch cubes, add salt and pepper to taste, a pinch of monosodium glutamate, the oil and sherry. Shake in the flour. Coat the meat with the batter and fry in hot oil until golden brown. Meanwhile, make the sauce by blending cornflour with sugar, salt and pepper and soy sauce, then add water or pineapple syrup. Boil until thick and clear.

Put pork in dish, top with vegetables and sauce.

Spicy Meat Balls   China

4–6 servings

½ teaspoon peppercorns
  (Chinese if available)
1 lb fat pork, minced
½ teaspoon salt
1 teaspoon sugar
3 tablespoons soy sauce

2 tablespoons dry sherry
2 teaspoons minced ginger
2 teaspoons minced spring
  onion
1 teaspoon cornflour
Oil

Heat the peppercorns in a pan, remove and crush with a rolling pin and sieve. Mix all the ingredients together and form into small balls. Fry in hot oil until brown. Drain, then re-fry for 1 minute to crisp.

Beef Shreds

China

Chao Nui Jou Szu

4 servings

8–10 oz fillet steak
2 teaspoons cornflour
2 tablespoons water
1 egg white
Salt and pepper
2 oz lard for frying
8 oz bean shoots

3 oz bamboo shoots
1 small onion
Small piece celery
2 tablespoons chicken stock
2 tablespoons soy sauce
1 tablespoon dry sherry
2 teaspoons sugar

Cut the steak into thin strips. Mix the cornflour with the water, unbeaten egg white and seasoning. Mix the beef with this. Fry in the hot lard until meat is crisp and brown, but lightly cooked.

Meanwhile, shred all the vegetables for the sauce very finely and heat in a pan with the stock, soy sauce and sherry. Add the sugar and additional salt and pepper to taste. Put the sauce at the bottom of the dish and top with the crisply fried steak.

Date Balls   Korea

Cho-raan

Makes 24 balls

1 lb dates	1–2 teaspoon(s) cinnamon
2 oz sugar	2 oz pine nuts, chopped

Remove the stones from the dates. Put into a basin in a steamer over boiling water and heat for 30 minutes until soft enough to mash or sieve. Mix with the sugar and cinnamon. Form into small balls and roll in chopped nuts.

Serve as a final course with tea or coffee.

Lamb Tails   China

Cha Yang Wei

5–6 servings

5 tablespoons caster sugar	1½ oz cornflour
1 tablespoon flour	2½ tablespoons water
2 tablespoons water	Oil for deep frying
3 egg whites, beaten until stiff	Icing sugar

Mix sugar, flour and 2 tablespoons water, form into 5–6 balls. Blend egg whites with the cornflour and water. Heat oil until it bubbles. Dip balls into the batter, then coat further by spreading batter with a spoon. Put each ball in oil and fry until deep golden brown. Be careful that oil does not get too hot.

Place on a dish and sprinkle with the sugar. Serve immediately.

India

India

India is a vast sub-continent but, wherever you go, curry is sure to be on the menu. However, the number of different curries is legion, mild, medium or hot; dry, moist or covered with sauce. None taste exactly the same. But with the curry are served a number of side dishes, sweet or hot or savoury, each one adding piquancy to the whole meal. A list of these is given on page 167.

Mulligatawny   India

4 servings

2 teaspoons turmeric
2 crushed cloves garlic
1 teaspoon mustard
2–3 chillis or
   ½ teaspoon chilli powder
   (optional)

Salt and crushed
   peppercorns
1½–2 pints mutton stock
2 onions, chopped
2 oz clarified butter (ghee)*

* In Indian cooking, butter is heated, then allowed to cool so that you
have pure fat.

*Make the basic stock, blend the spices and seasoning together.
Put into a pan with the mutton stock, and simmer for 20 minutes,
then strain. Meanwhile, fry the onions in the clarified butter until
soft. Add to the strained stock and simmer for a further 10
minutes. Serve with boiled rice, if liked.*

Cooking Rice

*Boiled rice is essential to serve with curries and other Indian and
Asiatic dishes. To be perfect, the rice must be white, with every
grain separated. Use a hard long-grain rice (Patna type). There
are two methods of cooking – one is found on page 140 in which
one measure of rice is cooked with 2 measures of water and salt
to taste – the proportions are the same with or without the potato.
In this method there is no need to strain or rinse the rice.*

   *The second method is to use 4 oz rice to at least 2 pints water
and ½–1 teaspoon salt. Add the rice to the rapidly boiling water,
cook for 12 minutes, test to see if just cooked but not too soft.
Strain, rinse in cold water then put into a greased dish or on
paper on a flat dish. Reheat gently – or stand the strainer over a
pan of boiling water, cover and reheat for a short time.*

Kedgeree   India

4 servings

8 oz Patna rice
4 oz lentils
Salt and pepper
2 oz butter, melted
  (optional)

Little sliced ginger
  (optional)
Bay leaf (optional)

Put the Patna rice and lentils to soak for an hour in 3 pints water, then simmer with salt to taste until the lentils are quite tender, and have absorbed the liquid – about 1 hour. Top with melted butter, if wished. To give more flavour, add a little sliced ginger and a bay leaf as well as pepper to the rice mixture. Serve with chutney and yoghourt.

Rice Pulao with Peas   India

Marta Pulao

4 servings

6–7 oz Patna rice
1½ oz clarified butter
  (ghee)*
6 cloves
2 pieces cinnamon
½ teaspoon turmeric

1 teaspoon caraway seeds
Salt
8 oz peas
2 pints plus 2 tablespoons
  hot water

* In Indian cooking, butter is heated, then allowed to cool so that you have pure fat.

Soak Patna rice in cold water for 1 hour. Heat clarified butter in a heavy pan, put in cloves, cinnamon, turmeric and caraway seeds. Fry over low heat for 2 minutes. Add the drained rice, salt to taste and peas. Mix and fry gently for a few minutes, stirring all the time. Next add all the hot water. Mix thoroughly, bring to the boil. Cook in covered pan or transfer to covered casserole and cook in the centre of moderate oven for 30 minutes. This pulao goes well with meat and vegetable dishes.

Indian Vegetable Dishes

The parathas (see page 168) can be stuffed with one of the following fillings, rolled firmly and served at once or re-fried to give a very crisp outside.

Fillings
(a) Creamed potatoes or sweet potatoes mashed with fried onion and flavoured with spices such as cumin or ginger.
(b) Peas, cooked in a savoury mixture of onion, tomatoes and ginger.
(c) Very lightly cooked or raw chopped cauliflower flavoured with spices such as ginger, cumin or chilli powder.

Quite familiar vegetables – leeks, peas, beans – can be cooked in a similar curry sauce to that used for chicken (see page 165) or the vegetables can be blended with a savoury curry mixture made by frying chopped onions and garlic in butter, then adding some or all of the spices used for the curry sauce.
  Because the mixture is dry, however, it will be very pungent, so care must be taken not to over-spice.

Mashed Aubergines India

Brinjal Bhurtha

4–6 servings

4 large aubergines
1 onion, chopped
2 green peppers, de-seeded
  and chopped

Juice of 1 lemon
Little oil

Boil or bake the aubergines, remove skin and mash the pulp. Mix the onion and green peppers with the lemon juice. Add the aubergine pulp and moisten with a little oil. Either heat gently or serve cold with curry.

Curries

The following chicken curry is an excellent example of a moist Indian curry.

Chicken Curry

India

4–6 servings

1 chicken, jointed
2 oz butter
1 small onion, chopped
1 small apple, peeled, cored
  and chopped
1 tablespoon curry powder
$\frac{1}{2}$ oz flour
1 teaspoon curry paste
1 pint stock
1 or 2 chillis (optional)
Good pinch powdered
  ginger

Good pinch powdered
  turmeric
1 tablespoon chutney
Squeeze lemon juice
Salt and pepper
2 oz desiccated coconut
1 oz sultanas
Thin rings of lightly fried,
  onion, green pepper,
  lemon rind and a few bay
  leaves

Fry the chicken pieces in hot butter, remove from pan. Fry the onion and apple for a few minutes, then add the curry powder, flour and curry paste. Cook for 2–3 minutes, then carefully blend in most of the stock. Bring to the boil and cook until a thin sauce. Add spices, chutney, lemon juice, seasoning and the chicken pieces. Pour remaining stock over the coconut, allow this to stand for a while, then add strained liquid to the curry. Add sultanas and simmer very gently for 2–3 hours. Garnish with the onion rings, green pepper, rind and bay leaves and serve with boiled rice.

Variations

Meat Curry

India

Use 1$\frac{1}{2}$ lb diced beef, mutton or other uncooked meat. If using cooked meat, then make the curry sauce and add the meat after the sauce has been cooking for some little time.

Fish Curry   India

Make the sauce and add diced uncooked fish about 30 minutes
before serving, and heat gently so the fish is not broken.

Home-made Curry Powder   India

½ teaspoon powdered
  cinnamon
½ teaspoon ground ginger
½ teaspoon turmeric
¼ teaspoon powdered
  chillis

½ teaspoon powdered cumin
Good pinch of powdered
  cloves
Good pinch saffron
½ teaspoon powdered
  coriander

Mix all ingredients well and store in an airtight container in a
dark place.

Lentil Curry   India

4 servings

8 oz lentils
1 onion, chopped
1 clove garlic, crushed
  (optional)
2 oz clarified butter
  (ghee)*
½ tablespoon curry powder

1 good tablespoon tomato
  paste or 3 skinned
  tomatoes
Stock or water
Pinch salt
Good pinch sugar

* In Indian cooking, butter is heated, then allowed to cool so that you
have pure fat.

166

Soak lentils for several hours or overnight in cold water. Fry onion and garlic in the butter with the curry powder. Add drained lentils, tomato paste or tomatoes, blended with a little stock or water, seasoning and sugar. Stir well together. Add enough liquid to cover, simmer gently for about 30 minutes until lentils are tender.

Variations:
Dried fruit, shredded coconut or chilli powder may be added.
  In place of curry powder use ½ teaspoon powdered turmeric, ½ teaspoon chilli powder plus a pinch powdered ginger.

Side Dishes to Serve with Curries   India

Chutney

Chapati
These flat Indian cakes can be served with rice, but generally accompany a curry if no rice is being cooked. They are available in shops stocking Indian food.
  Sieve 4 oz wholemeal flour and pinch salt. Blend with enough water to give a stiff dough. Divide into lumps the size of a large egg. Roll out thinly to size and shape of a pancake. Bake on a griddle or frying-pan.
  The bread is pressed with a cloth before being removed from the griddle so that it fills with air and automatically punctures.

Paratha
Ingredients as above. Mix dough, divide into lumps and roll out thinly. Spread each piece with butter. Fry in butter on griddle or frying-pan.

Chopped Chillis
Use these sparingly, as they are very hot.

Chopped Fresh Herbs
Mix with a little sugar.

Pickles
Gherkins, sliced or whole, pickled red cabbage or pickled onions.

Fruit
Sliced banana, apple or lemon, shredded or desiccated coconut.

Sliced Peppers
Both green and red peppers can be used.

Bombay Duck
This strong-smelling dried fish is delicious on curries. It can be fried in a little fat, or baked in the oven until crisp and then crumbled over the curry.

Indian Desserts

Yoghourt, sweetened and flavoured with spices like cinnamon, is an excellent sweet to follow a curry.

Carrot Kheer   India

4 servings

12 oz carrots, peeled and   Pinch saffron
 grated   Pinch powdered cinnamon
1½ pints milk   2–3 oz cashew nuts,
1–2 oz sugar   chopped

Cook the carrots in the milk with the sugar, until tender. Add the
saffron, cinnamon and the chopped cashew nuts. Serve cold
with cream.

Semolina Cream   India

Halva Suji

4–6 servings

1¼ pints milk   2 oz blanched almonds,
6 oz sugar   chopped
¼ pint water   3 oz raisins
2 oz butter   1 teaspoon ground
4 oz semolina   cardamom
                                 1 teaspoon cinnamon

Put the milk, sugar and water into a pan. Heat slowly, stirring
occasionally, until sugar is dissolved. Meanwhile, slowly melt
butter in another pan. Add semolina, almonds and raisins. Cook,
stirring, over low heat until golden. Stir milk mixture into semo-
lina mixture. Add cardamom and cinnamon, mixing well. Bring
to the boil, stirring. Reduce heat, simmer covered until the liquid
is absorbed – about 5 minutes. Remove from heat, cool slightly.
Spoon into dishes. Serve warm with cream, if liked.

Africa

South, Central and West Africa

Africa abounds in tropical fruits and vegetables.

There are interesting ways of cooking chicken (see page 179), frying fish (see page 178), and pickling fish (see page 177).

Bananas are used a great deal in cooking, a favourite is Banana Pudding (see page 183).

The dishes of South Africa reflect past European interest in the country, for instance, Roast Pork with Apple and Raisin Sauce (see page 181).

Corn or Mealie Soup South and Central Africa

4–6 servings

2 large fresh corn cobs or
    12 oz canned or frozen
    corn
$1\frac{1}{4}$ pints milk
4 oz butter

1 onion, finely chopped
1 oz flour
Salt and pepper
2 slices bread

Simmer fresh or frozen corn steadily for about 15–20 minutes, adding a little salt towards the end of the cooking time. Cool, then strip the kernels from the cob.

Save about $\frac{1}{4}$ pint of the liquid in which the corn was cooked, adding a little extra milk or water if necessary to bring this up to $\frac{1}{4}$ pint – add to the milk. Heat half the butter in a pan and fry the finely chopped onion. Stir in the flour and cook for several minutes.

Add liquid gradually, bring to the boil, stirring to prevent burning. Cook until slightly thickened and smooth.

Put in the corn and season with salt and pepper to taste. Reheat. Serve with bread cut into small croûtons and fried in remaining butter.

Avocado Pears South Africa

Avocado pears are one of the most typical South African fruits. The following are some of the ways in which avocados can be served.

1. Cut the avocado in half lengthways and take out the stone. Cover the flesh with a little lemon juice to keep it from going brown. Fill centre with a mixture of shredded lettuce, sliced hard-boiled egg, sliced tomato and anchovy fillets.
2. Squeeze lemon juice over flesh. Fill with a mixture of diced sweet pepper, diced pineapple and chopped prawns. Garnish with anchovy fillets.
3. Simply serve the avocado pears with a good oil and vinegar dressing.
4. Fill the centre with shellfish in a tomato-flavoured mayonnaise.
5. Remove the pulp and chop neatly into cubes. Toss with lemon juice and add to diced chicken, mix well and pile on to a bed of shredded lettuce in the shell.

Vegetables in Africa

Some of the most popular are:

Aubergines, which can be stuffed or sliced, floured and fried.

Mealies or corn, which are very plentiful in South Africa and are cooked by stripping off the outer leaves and cooking the cob in boiling water for 15 minutes, salting towards the end of the cooking time. The younger the corn the shorter the time of cooking.

Pumpkin, which is served boiled or mashed, or mashed and made into fritters.

Yams, or sweet potatoes, which are available throughout Africa and are boiled, mashed or roasted like ordinary potatoes.

Savoury Fritters   South Africa

4–6 servings

8 oz mashed pumpkin
2 eggs
Salt and pepper

4 oz self-raising flour
Fat for frying

*Mix together all ingredients except fat. Fry in hot fat until crisp
and brown.*

*For sweet fritters add a little cinnamon, 2 oz sugar, and when
fried, top with sliced lemon and sugar.*

Stuffed Aubergines   Central Africa

4 servings

**Garden egg is the name used in parts of Africa for aubergine.
Egg plant is another name.**

2 large aubergines
2 oz fat or peanut butter
1 onion, chopped (optional)
8 oz lamb or beef, minced
2 tomatoes
½ teaspoon salt

¼ teaspoon cayenne pepper
  (optional)
2 oz breadcrumbs
2–3 tablespoon dried
  breadcrumbs
1 oz fat

Wash aubergines and cut in half. Scoop out pulp, leaving a thin shell. Dice pulp and cook in the fat or peanut butter over a low heat until soft. Add onion if liked. Mix together the rest of the ingredients except the crumbs and fat, and fill the aubergine shells. Sprinkle with crumbs and top with fat – brown in a hot oven or under the grill.

Fish in Africa

One of the most famous fish dishes of South Africa is pickled fish (see page 177). Crab stew (see page 177) and highly seasoned fried fish (see page 178) are typical of Ghana. Around the coast of South Africa there are snoek, an oily fish, best dried and smoked; stock-fish, a very tender white fish, harder, rather like a herring but firmer; kobbeljauw, which resembles cod. Fruit is sometimes added to fish (see page 176).

Grilled Fish with Orange Butter   South Africa

4 servings

1 onion, chopped
2 oz butter
Grated rind of ½ orange
    and juice of 1 orange

4 white fish
2 whole oranges, cut into
    bite-sized pieces

Fry onion in half the butter, add the orange rind and orange juice. Melt rest of butter and brush fish with this. Grill until nearly done, the time depends on the type of fish, then add orange pieces and reheat. Serve fish topped with orange pieces with the delicious orange butter spooned over.

Crab Stew   Ghana

4 servings

4 small or 1 large crab
1 oz butter
8 oz tomatoes, chopped
1 onion, finely chopped
½ teaspoon powdered
  ginger

Cayenne pepper
Salt
¼ pint water

*Clean 4 small or 1 large crab, boil and dress. Alternatively, buy
ready-cooked and dressed crabs. Remove flesh; clean, polish and
reserve shell.*

*Heat butter in a pan. Fry tomatoes and onion until cooked.
Add ginger, little cayenne pepper, salt to taste, the water and
crabmeat and simmer gently, stirring, until heated through. Add
more water if necessary.*

*Put crab mixture into shell. Serve with boiled rice and
mashed yams or sweet potatoes.*

Pickled Fish   South Africa

8–10 servings

3 lb thick fillets of white
  fish
2 oz flour seasoned with
  1 teaspoon salt and good
  pinch black pepper and
  good pinch cayenne
  pepper
Fat for frying
1½ pints white or malt
  vinegar

Peppercorns or use 1
  tablespoon mixed
  pickling spice for hotter
  flavour
1½ oz flour
1 tablespoon curry powder
3 bay leaves
1 large onion, thinly sliced

Cut the fish into neat slices. Coat with the seasoned flour and fry in hot fat until just cooked but unbroken. Heat 1 pint vinegar with a few peppercorns or pickling spices for about 5 minutes. Strain. Blend the flour and the curry powder with the remaining ½ pint vinegar, add the hot strained vinegar and cook, stirring well, until it is a smooth sauce. Arrange the fish in a dish with the bay leaves, thinly sliced onion, then cover with the vinegar sauce. Keep in a cool place for 2–3 days so that the fish absorbs all the flavours.

Seasoned Fried Fish   Central Africa/Ghana

4 servings

1 large bream or other
   suitable fish, herring,
   mackerel, plaice, sole
Salt and pepper
Flour

6 oz peanut butter or oil
8 oz onions, chopped
12 oz tomatoes, skinned and
   chopped

Wash the fish and cut into four. Sprinkle with plenty of salt and pepper. Toss in flour. Fry in hot peanut butter or oil until golden brown on both sides. Drain and keep hot. Fry onions lightly in the hot fish fat. Add tomatoes and cook for a further few minutes. Season. Arrange fish portions as a whole on an oval dish. Lay onion and tomato mixture on top. Pour over remaining butter or oil.

Chicken in Orange Almond Sauce   South Africa

4 servings

1 young chicken
$\frac{1}{4}$ teaspoon salt
3 oz butter
1 oz flour
Pinch each of salt,
   cinnamon and ginger

$\frac{3}{4}$ pint orange juice
2 oz blanched almonds,
   sliced
2 oz seedless raisins
2 oranges, peeled and
   segmented

Joint the chicken, or ask your butcher to do it. Sprinkle with the salt. Melt the butter in a saucepan and brown chicken lightly, then remove it from the pan. Mix the flour with the salt, cinnamon and powdered ginger. Blend with butter in pan to make a smooth paste. Add the orange juice, cook, stirring constantly, until sauce bubbles and begins to thicken. Return chicken to pan with the almonds and raisins. Cover and cook over a low heat until the chicken is tender – approximately 30 minutes. Add the orange segments and heat through.

Serve chicken and sauce on a bed of plain boiled rice.

Ashanti Fowl   Ghana

6 servings

One 5-lb roasting chicken,
   boned
8 oz onions, chopped
12 oz tomatoes, skinned and
   chopped
8 oz peanut butter

2 oz breadcrumbs
Salt
Pinch of cayenne pepper
Fat
Flour

S–WC–I

Ask your butcher to bone the chicken, if possible.

For the stuffing, fry the onions and tomatoes in the peanut butter. Add the breadcrumbs, pinch of salt and cayenne pepper.

Lay boned chicken flat on a board, sprinkle with salt, cover with prepared stuffing. Tie into a neat shape, cover with a little fat, sprinkle lightly with flour.

Roast for 1½ hours in a hot oven until crisp and golden brown.

Meats in Africa

Throughout Africa, lamb and mutton are better and more plentiful than beef. Pork and bacon are used in some parts. Bacon is sometimes fried with aubergines.

Fricadels   South Africa

4 servings

2 oz bread	2 eggs, beaten
2 or 3 tablespoons warm milk or tomato juice	Good pinch mixed herbs
	Salt and pepper
1 lb uncooked lamb or beef, minced	Grated nutmeg (optional)
	Crisp breadcrumbs
1 onion, grated or minced	Fat for frying

Cut off and discard the crusts from the bread, pour over the warm milk or tomato juice. Then allow to stand for a little while. Beat until smooth and add the minced meat together with the onion, half the eggs, the herbs, salt and pepper to taste and nutmeg, if used. Form into small balls the size of a walnut. Roll in the remaining beaten egg and the crisp breadcrumbs. Fry steadily in the fat until cooked and golden brown.

Bobotie

4–6 servings

1 oz dripping or fat
2 onions, chopped
1 tablespoon curry powder
1 teaspoon salt
2 teaspoons sugar
1 tablespoon vinegar or
  lemon juice

1 apple, sliced (optional)
2 thick slices of bread
½ pint milk
Few chopped almonds
2 oz sultanas
1½ lb minced lamb
2 small eggs

Heat fat in a pan, cook chopped onions until soft, add curry powder, salt, sugar, vinegar or lemon juice and apple; mix thoroughly. Put bread into a dish, pour over the milk and allow to stand for 15 minutes. Pour off any milk not absorbed and reserve. Beat the bread until very soft, add this to the fried onion mixture, together with the almonds, sultanas, lamb and 1 of the eggs. Put into a well-greased dish. Pour the reserved milk over the second egg, cover the meat mixture with this custard. Put the dish into the middle of a moderately hot oven and cook for 30 minutes. After this time reduce the heat to very moderate for a further 30 minutes.

Roast Pork with Apple and Raisin Sauce
South Africa/Rhodesia

4–6 servings

3 lb loin of pork
Salt and pepper
½ pint cider

1 lb small white onions
  whole, but skinned

Trim excess fat from the meat. Sprinkle generously with salt and pepper. Put on a rack in a shallow baking tin. Roast in a slow oven allowing 35–40 minutes to the pound. Baste frequently with the cider. Meanwhile, simmer the onions for 30 minutes in salted water.

Half an hour before meat has finished cooking, place onions round joint, and continue baking. Serve pork with Apple and Raisin Sauce.

Apple and Raisin Sauce   South Africa/Rhodesia

1 lb apples
1 tablespoon sugar
2 oz seedless raisins

Little lemon juice
$\frac{1}{2}$ teaspoon powdered ginger

Peel, core and slice the apples. Add the rest of the ingredients and cook until the apples are soft and fluffy – about 10 minutes. Serve with roast pork.

Fruit in Africa

Fruits abound in South Africa and in many other parts of Africa; oranges, lemons, pears, pineapple and grapes many of which are exported. Grenadilla (passion fruit), paw-paw, melon, guava, mangoes are served raw or used in various dishes.

Banana Pudding

4 servings

4 large bananas
2 tablespoons brown sugar
Juice 1 orange

2 oz fresh coconut or 1 oz
  desiccated coconut

Peel bananas and arrange in a buttered dish. Mix sugar and orange juice and pour over bananas. Sprinkle thickly with coconut. Bake in a moderately hot oven for 20 minutes until bananas are soft and the coconut is brown.

Ground-nut (Peanut) cakes

Central Africa

10–12 cakes

8 oz shelled peanuts
8 oz sugar
1 tablespoon butter or
  peanut butter (optional)

1 tablespoon water
Pinch caraway seeds or
  aniseed (optional)

Heat peanuts in a hot oven for a few minutes, rub off skins, return to oven for 5 minutes. Dissolve sugar, and butter if liked, in the water. Boil without stirring until golden brown and thick like toffee. Add peanuts and mix well, add seeds, if liked. Pour into buttered tin and mark into flat cakes or place on a wet board and cut into fancy shapes before mixture becomes too cool and hardens.

Orange Cream Pie — South Africa

4–6 servings

8-inch baked pastry case
6 oz sugar
1 oz cornflour
Grated rind of $\frac{1}{2}$ orange
and juice 1 orange made
up to $\frac{1}{2}$ pint with water

1 tablespoon lemon juice
$\frac{1}{2}$ oz butter
2 egg yolks, beaten
$\frac{1}{4}$ pint double cream,
whipped
1 orange, sliced

Prepare and bake the pastry case.

Mix the sugar, cornflour, orange rind and lemon juice together smoothly. Heat the orange juice and water mixture with the butter. Add the blended cornflour, cook for 3 minutes, stirring constantly. Add the beaten egg yolks, cook for 1–2 minutes without boiling. When cold, beat well, then fold in the whipped cream. Pile into pastry case, decorate with orange slices.

Passion Fruit Cream — South Africa

4 servings

$\frac{1}{2}$ oz powdered gelatine
4 tablespoons water
$\frac{1}{4}$ pint fresh orange juice
Generous $\frac{1}{4}$ pint passion
fruit pulp

$\frac{1}{2}$ pint double cream or
evaporated milk, lightly
whipped
2 egg whites, stiffly beaten
1 orange, cut into slices

Soften the gelatine in the water, and dissolve over a pan of very hot water. Stir in the orange juice and the passion fruit pulp, sieved to remove the pips if wished. Cool, then fold in whipped cream or evaporated milk, and the beaten egg whites. Pile on a dish and decorate with slices of fresh orange.

North America

North America

North America is one of the richest sources of recipes. From the time of the earliest settlers, people from the 'Old World' have brought their ways of living to enrich the traditions of the New World.

One of the heritages of the wagon trail is that everything is still measured in cups and spoons rather than pounds and ounces. But I have used the latter throughout the book. However there is a conversion table on pages x–xii.

Lobster Chowder USA

4 servings

1 small boiled lobster
1 pint water
1–2 rashers bacon
1 teaspoon finely chopped
   onion
1½ oz flour

1 potato, diced
⅜ pint milk and cream or
   cream
Good pinch sugar
Salt and pepper

Remove flesh from lobster, put shell into pan with the water and simmer gently for about 15 minutes. Strain and make up to 1 pint again with water. Cut rind from bacon, and then cut into narrow strips. Fry lightly adding onion and flour and cook gently without letting it brown.* Gradually add the lobster stock, stirring all the time. When it comes to the boil and thickens, add the lobster cut into small pieces, the diced potato and the remaining ingredients. Either reduce heat under pan or put in a double saucepan and cook until a thick creamy mixture. Serve with crisp toast.

* If using very lean bacon add scant 1 oz butter before adding onion and flour.

Hors d'oeuvres

These vary a great deal – they can be fruit or fruit juices or delicious salads at which Americans excel.

   Shellfish cocktails are another excellent choice – these are made by blending a little tomato purée, Tabasco and Worcestershire sauce with mayonnaise, then tossing prawns, crabmeat or lobster in this and serving on shredded lettuce in glasses kept cool over ice.

Salads are a joy to look at in America for fruits are combined with the usual salad ingredients.

One of the most interesting salads is a Waldorf salad. Combine diced apples, celery and chopped nuts with mayonnaise – serve on a bed of green salad.

Coleslaw combines shredded cabbage, shredded carrot (or grated), chopped nuts, grated apple and chopped celery with mayonnaise or oil, vinegar and seasoning.

The proportions of ingredients in these two salads can be adjusted to your taste.

King Crab Mayonnaise USA

4–6 servings

Large dressed crab or
   large can or large packet
   frozen crabmeat
1 medium onion, chopped
1 tablespoon oil
$\frac{1}{2}$ tablespoon curry powder
$\frac{1}{2}$ tablespoon tomato purée
1 tablespoon honey

4 fl oz red wine
3 fl oz water
Salt
Juice $\frac{1}{2}$ lemon
$\frac{1}{2}$ pint mayonnaise
5–6 tomatoes, sliced
12 black olives, stoned and
   chopped

Arrange crabmeat in long serving dish. Fry onion in hot oil for 3–4 minutes. Add curry powder and cook for a further 2 minutes. Add tomato purée, honey, wine and water. Bring to the boil, season with salt and add lemon juice. Simmer for 10–15 minutes until it has become thick and syrupy. Strain and leave to cool. Stir into mayonnaise and spoon over crabmeat. Garnish with a border of tomato slices and small pieces black olives.

Chilli Con Carne

3–4 servings

2 oz margarine or oil
1 onion
1 red or green pepper
2–3 sticks celery (optional)
1–4 teaspoons chilli powder
8 oz haricot beans, soaked
    and cooked

½ teaspoon salt
1 lb minced beef
8 oz tomatoes, skinned and
    chopped
¼ pint stock or water
Raw onion rings

Heat margarine or oil in a pan, then fry a chopped onion and pepper and several sticks of celery (optional). Cook until vegetables are tender. Add chilli powder (latter amount correct, but it's very hot so adjust to personal taste), haricot beans, salt, minced beef, skinned chopped tomatoes and water or stock. Cover the pan and simmer very gently for 30 minutes, add extra water or stock if needed, but remember this should be a very thick stew. Continue cooking for about 25 minutes. Garnish with raw onion rings.

Brownies

USA

Makes 20

4 oz butter
4 oz plain chocolate
4 eggs

6 oz caster sugar
4 oz self-raising flour
4 oz chopped nuts

Put the butter and the chocolate into a basin over hot water. Heat until chocolate has melted. Beat the eggs and sugar together until thick and light. Fold the chocolate mixture into the egg mixture, then add the flour and nuts.

Line a Swiss-roll tin with very well-greased greaseproof paper. Pour in the mixture and bake for about 40 minutes in the centre of a very moderate oven. Test by pressing firmly on top, the cake should be quite firm. Turn out and cut into fingers.

Brownies should be rather soft and sticky in the middle, so do not overcook.

Honey, Date and Walnut Cake

Canada and USA

10–12 servings

8 oz flour (with plain flour use 3 teaspoons baking powder; with self-raising flour use 1 teaspoon baking powder)
Pinch salt
4 oz butter

4 oz caster sugar
4 oz sliced stoned dates
1 oz chopped walnuts
2 eggs
4 tablespoons milk
2 tablespoons clear honey

Sieve the flour, baking powder and salt into a bowl, rub in the butter. Add the sugar, dates and walnuts, mix to a soft consistency with eggs, milk and honey. Put into a greased 7-inch square tin, bake in centre of a moderate oven for 1–1¼ hours. Serve fresh as a cake or as bread, spread with butter and honey.

Honey Muffins   Canada and USA

Makes 10 large or 20 small

1 lb flour (with plain
  flour use 3 teaspoons
  baking powder)
1 teaspoon salt
$\frac{1}{2}$ pint milk

4 tablespoons honey
1 egg, beaten
2 oz melted fat
Butter

Sieve flour, or flour and baking powder, and salt. Mix milk, honey and egg and stir into dry ingredients with melted fat. Half-fill large, greased deep bun or muffin tins with the mixture and bake towards the top of a moderately hot oven for 25–30 minutes. Serve while warm with butter.

Johnny Cake   Canada

Makes 8–10 slices

Ground maize was used a great deal by early settlers, but use rice or cornflour or a mixture of ordinary flour and cornflour.

4 oz black treacle (molasses)
3 oz fat
1 level teaspoon bicarbonate
  of soda

$\frac{1}{2}$ pint sour milk or fresh
  milk plus few drops
  vinegar
8 oz ground maize or flour

Heat black treacle and fat together until melted. Blend the bicarbonate of soda with the sour milk. Beat both into the maize or flour. Pour into a well-greased 8-inch cake tin and bake in the centre of a moderate oven for about 40–45 minutes until pale golden brown. Turn out and eat hot with butter.

Caribbean and
West Indies

Caribbean and West Indies

Tropical fruits, including coconuts, pineapple, paw-paw, passion fruit, guavas together with an excellent selection of tropical vegetables and fish contribute to the colourful menus in this part of the world.

Many recipes have been brought to these islands by the ancestors of the present-day inhabitants – so dishes range from European, particularly Spanish, to Chinese and African. Rum, which is made in the West Indies, is used in many dishes.

Avocado and Crab Soup Caribbean/West Indies

4 servings

Avocado pears abound in these islands, and this delicious soup is made by combining them with shellfish.

1 onion, chopped
1–2 cloves garlic, chopped
2 oz butter
$\frac{1}{2}$ oz flour
1$\frac{1}{2}$ pints chicken stock

2 avocado pears, peeled, stoned and chopped
1 boiled crab
$\frac{1}{4}$ pint single cream

Fry the onion and garlic in the butter. Stir in the flour, then add the stock (which can be given additional flavour by simmering the crab shell in it for 15 minutes before adding to the onion mixture). Bring to the boil, then add the avocado flesh and crabmeat, stir well and add the cream.

Ground-nut Soup   Caribbean/West Indies

6 servings

3 onions, sliced
3 tomatoes, peeled and sliced
1 avocado pear, peeled, stoned and sliced
2 oz peanut butter

1$\frac{1}{2}$ pints chicken stock
2 oz nuts, finely chopped
Salt and pepper
4 oz chicken meat (optional)

This is a rather more elaborate soup than that on page 195.

Fry the onions, tomatoes and avocado in the peanut butter.
Add the chicken stock, chopped nuts and salt and pepper to taste,
and chicken, if wished.

Bring to the boil and simmer until the vegetables are tender,
about 15 minutes.

Jambalaya   West Indies

4–6 servings

2 onions, chopped
2 cloves garlic
2 oz butter
4 tomatoes, skinned and
   chopped
1 lb cooked sausages,
   diced, or whole peeled
   prawns

1 green pepper or red
   pepper, chopped
Pinch of chilli powder
   (optional)
6–8 oz cooked long-grain
   rice

Fry the onions and 1–2 cloves garlic in the butter. Add the
tomatoes and cook until the tomatoes are pulped. Add the
sausages or prawns, and the sweet pepper plus a little chilli
powder, if liked. Add the cooked rice. Mix well. Heat all ingredients together.

Baked Bananas in Coconut

Caribbean/West Indies

Follow the recipe for Banana Pudding (see page 183), but add a little rum to the orange juice.

Sweet Potato Pudding

Caribbean/West Indies

3 oz sweet potatoes or yams,
    cooked and mashed
3 oz butter
6 oz sugar
1 egg
4–6 oz dried fruit

$\frac{1}{2}$ teaspoon mixed spice
$\frac{1}{2}$ pint coconut cream or
    2 oz desiccated coconut
    and 1 small can
    evaporated milk or $\frac{1}{4}$ pint
    thin cream

Blend the sweet potatoes with the butter and sugar. Add the egg, dried fruit, mixed spice and coconut cream, or use 2 oz desiccated coconut and evaporated milk. Put into a greased pie dish and cook for 1 hour in the centre of a very moderate oven until just set.

Apples and Rum

Caribbean

4 servings

2 oz sugar
Scant $\frac{1}{4}$ pint water

1 lb apples, peeled, cored
    and sliced
Rum

Heat the sugar and water together to make a syrup. Cook the apples in the syrup and flavour with rum to taste.

Pineapple Pancakes   Caribbean

4 servings

Fresh pineapple, peeled, cored and diced
Sugar
Marmalade or jam

8 pancakes, made your usual way (or see pages 52 or 115)

Mix the pineapple with sugar to taste, add marmalade or jam of choice. Put aside whilst you make the pancakes. Fill each pancake with the pineapple mixture and serve hot.

Baked Pineapple   Caribbean

4 servings

1 whole pineapple, peeled and cored

Brown sugar
Rum (optional)

Coat the whole pineapple with brown sugar and bake in a moderate oven for 30 minutes, spooning over more sugar as it cooks. Flambé the pineapple with rum, if wished. Slice the pineapple before cooking, if preferred.

Baked Oranges   Caribbean

4 servings

4 oranges	2 oz brown sugar
Boiling water	Rum to taste
1 oz butter	$\frac{1}{4}$ pint cream

Cover the oranges with boiling water, leave until cool, then remove peel. (This method means all the pith can be easily removed together with the centre core.) Put into a deep dish, with the butter, brown sugar and rum. Bake in the centre of a moderate oven for 15–20 minutes. Serve with fresh cream.

Australasia

Australia and New Zealand

While much of the food in these countries is based on British country fare, during the years it has altered. The influence of migrants from many other European countries, and the proximity of the East with its exotic dishes now shows. Both countries have excellent dairy produce, and Australia in particular has a wealth of tropical fruit. Meat, fish and vegetables are of excellent quality, and obtainable in profusion except in the more desolate 'outback' areas.

Pumpkin is a vegetable much used by Australian housewives both as a savoury and sweet.

Avocado Chicken Soup   Australia

4 servings

2 ripe avocado pears
$\frac{1}{4}$ pint white wine
1$\frac{1}{2}$ pints chicken soup

Salt and pepper
Grated cheese

Peel and stone the avocados and cut the flesh into thin slices. Cover with the wine and leave for a short time, then add to the hot soup and simmer for a few minutes only, season to taste with salt and pepper. Spoon into hot soup bowls and garnish with a little grated cheese.

Kangaroo Tail Soup   Australia

Oxtail can be used instead of kangaroo tail – there is no need to leave this standing – just prepare and cook.

6 servings

2 tablespoons oil or fat
2 tablespoons vinegar or
    lemon juice
3 pints water
Salt and pepper
2 bay leaves
Pinch nutmeg
Pinch cayenne
1 kangaroo tail, cut in neat
    pieces

2 onions, chopped
2 carrots, diced
1 turnip diced
2–3 sticks celery, chopped
2 oz flour
$\frac{1}{4}$ pint red wine or water
Chopped parsley

Put oil or fat in a pan, immediately add the vinegar or lemon juice and water with the seasonings and spices. Put on to heat. Add the tail and allow to stand, if possible, for 48 hours.

Then add vegetables and simmer gently until tender. Take meat off the bones, return meat to pan. Blend flour with wine or water and stir into the soup. Bring just to the boil and simmer gently until thickened. Garnish with parsley.

Typical hors d'oeuvres

Oysters which are plentiful in many parts of Australia.
Shellfish cocktails made from chopped oysters, mussels, flaked crayfish or crab in tomato-flavoured mayonnaise.
Avocado pears are served with an oil and vinegar dressing, or filled with shellfish in mayonnaise.
Fresh fruit including grapefruit, melon, paw-paw and various fruit juices are also popular.

Meat in Australia and New Zealand

Both these countries produce large quantities of meat, in particular lamb and mutton, so it is not surprising they also consume a great deal of meat. In the past it was usual to serve steaks or chops for breakfast, but this custom is gradually dying out, particularly in the cities.

Because meat is of very high quality it can be served as roast, grilled and fried dishes, although meat pies are great favourites.

Carpet Bag Steak   Australia/New Zealand

The most usual way to serve this is to make a pocket in a large steak and put in half a dozen oysters with a little seasoning and butter, then grill or fry in the usual way.

The following recipe gives a more substantial stuffing suitable for a thick piece of topside or rump steak.

Carpet Bag Steak   Australia

8 servings

1½ oz butter
12–18 small oysters or
  mussels
4 oz mushrooms, sliced
6 oz white breadcrumbs
1 tablespoon chopped
  parsley

Grated rind of ½ lemon
Salt and pepper
1 egg, beaten
4-lb piece topside or rump
  beef

Heat butter and toss oysters and mushrooms in it for 5 minutes. Transfer to basin and mix in breadcrumbs, parsley, lemon rind, salt and pepper and beaten egg.

Slit the meat open on one side only. Press stuffing into the pocket in the steak. Sew or skewer edges together. Roast in a very moderate oven, to prevent shrinkage, for 2 hours.

Barbecues

These are as popular in Australasia as in America. Steaks, chops and sausages are cooked over a charcoal fire. To keep the meat moist brush it with melted butter or oil.

Spiced Barbecue Sauce Australia/New Zealand

1 tablespoon made mustard
2–3 tablespoons tomato
  purée or tomato ketchup
Few drops Worcestershire
  sauce

3 tablespoons oil
Little sugar or honey to
  taste

Blend all ingredients together. Put in a screw-top jar and use for basting as required. This is enough for 4 large or 8 small pieces of meat.

Colonial Goose   New Zealand

4 servings

1 large onion, finely
  chopped
Salt and pepper
4 oz fresh white
  breadcrumbs
4 rashers lean bacon,
  chopped

1 tablespoon each of
  chopped parsley, thyme,
  sage
1 egg
1 shoulder New Zealand
  lamb

Boil onion for a few minutes only in salted water. Strain and mix with salt and pepper to taste, breadcrumbs, bacon and herbs. Bind with the egg.

From the underneath side of the joint loosen flesh from the wide blade-bone end with a sharp pointed knife to make a cavity. Fill the cavity with some of the stuffing and sew or skewer the ends together to prevent the stuffing coming out.

Make the remainder of the stuffing into balls which may be cooked round the joint. Roast the joint in a moderate oven allowing 30 minutes per pound.

Vegetables and Fruit

Due to the great variation in climate in the various parts of Australasia, there is infinite variety in vegetables — ranging from sprouts, cauliflower and spinach to red and green peppers and aubergines. One of the most popular is pumpkin which is boiled and mashed as a vegetable, or used in scones, fritters or in a pie like the famous American pumpkin pie. Apples and pears are of excellent quality, so are passion fruit, citrus fruit and pineapple. Pineapple is used in many ways.

Passion Fruit Ice Cream   Australia

4 servings

¼ pint passion fruit pulp   caster sugar
¼ pint whipped cream   1 egg white, stiffly beaten

Blend the passion fruit pulp with the whipped cream. Add sugar to taste and the stiffly beaten egg white. Freeze as quickly as possible. Whip when half frozen to incorporate more air, then refreeze for several hours.

Pavlova Base

Australia/New Zealand

8 servings

4 egg whites	1 teaspoon cornflour
8 oz caster sugar	$\frac{1}{2}$–1 teaspoon white vinegar

Perhaps the most famous dessert from Australia and New Zealand. It is a meringue base or case, topped or filled with fruit and cream – often with passion fruit pulp blended with ice-cream. There are many versions.

Whisk the egg whites until very stiff, beat in half the caster sugar gradually, then fold in the remaining sugar mixed with the cornflour. Finally, add the vinegar.

Spread into a round or form into a flan shape on oiled or buttered paper on a baking sheet and bake in a slow oven for 3 hours or until meringue has completely dried out but is still pale in colour. Remove from paper and allow to cool. Store in an airtight tin until ready to fill. Fill with a mixture of ice cream and fruit, fresh or canned.

Anzacs

Makes 36

5 oz butter
1 level tablespoon golden
  syrup
1 teaspoon bicarbonate of
  soda

2 tablespoons boiling water
4 oz plain flour
4 oz rolled oats
4–6 oz sugar
4 oz raisins

These are also a favourite in Australia.

Melt the butter and golden syrup. Dissolve the bicarbonate of soda in the boiling water and add to butter and syrup. Mix together the plain flour, rolled oats, sugar and raisins before pouring the butter liquid on to them. Mix well. Place teaspoons of the mixture on a greased tray, allowing room for spreading. Bake in a slow oven for about 15 minutes. Do not remove from tray until slightly cool and set. Store in airtight tins when quite cold.

If liked, you can omit raisins and add desiccated coconut.

Lamingtons

Makes 16

5 oz butter
7 oz caster sugar
Vanilla essence
3 eggs
10 oz flour (with plain
  flour use 2½ teaspoons
  baking powder)

Pinch salt
4 tablespoons milk
Raspberry jam
7 oz icing sugar
1 oz cocoa
3 tablespoons boiling water
6 oz desiccated coconut

Cream the butter and sugar with a few drops of vanilla essence. Add the eggs gradually and beat well. Fold in the sieved flour and salt alternately with the milk.

Spread the mixture into a greased 8-inch square cake tin and bake for 50–60 minutes in the centre of a moderate oven. Cool and store in an airtight tin.

Next day slit the cake through the centre and spread with the raspberry jam. Place the 2 pieces together again and cut the cake into 2-inch squares. Put the icing sugar in a bowl, make a well in the centre and add the cocoa.

Pour the boiling water slowly on to it. Stir with a wooden spoon, gradually working in the icing sugar. Add more water if necessary. Keep the icing thin by standing it over hot water. Put a square of the cake on to the prongs of a fork or a skewer and dip into the chocolate icing, allow any excess to drip off. Toss in the coconut, and allow to set on a cake wire. Store in an airtight tin.

Pumpkin Scones   Australia/New Zealand

These can be either sweet or savoury.

4 oz self-raising flour
1 teaspoon baking powder
1 oz margarine
4 oz cooked pumpkin

Salt and pepper (for savoury scones)
1 oz sugar (for sweet scones)
Milk

Sieve together the flour and baking powder, rub in the margarine. Add the cooked pumpkin and mix with seasoning for savoury scones, or the sugar for sweet scones. Add milk to give a rolling consistency. Roll out to $\frac{1}{2}$-inch thickness, cut into rounds and bake on a greased baking sheet for 15 minutes towards the top of a hot oven.

Serve with plenty of butter.

Pumpkin Pie   Australia

6 servings

6 oz shortcrust pastry
12 oz cooked pumpkin
1 oz butter
2 eggs, separated

4 oz sugar
Juice and grated rind of 1
    lemon

Many American recipes are becoming popular in Australia, and
this is one of them.

Line a flan ring, tin or pie dish with the shortcrust pastry; bake
blind for 10 minutes. Sieve the cooked pumpkin, mix with the
butter, egg yolks, 2 oz sugar and grated lemon rind and juice.

Put into the pastry case and cook for 20–25 minutes in centre
of moderately hot oven. Whisk the egg whites until very stiff,
gradually add the remaining sugar. Pile the egg-white mixture
on pumpkin mixture and brown for 15 minutes in a very moderate oven. Serve hot.

Spice or cinnamon, with a little milk, could be used instead of
lemon.

Iced Sultana Loaf   Australia/New Zealand

8–10 servings

4 oz butter
4 oz caster sugar
2 eggs, beaten
8 oz self-raising flour or
    plain flour and 2
    teaspoons baking powder

6 oz sultanas
Milk to mix
6–8 oz icing sugar
Water to mix
10 walnut halves
1–2 oz sultanas

Cream the butter and sugar together until light. Add the beaten eggs slowly. Fold in the sieved flour or flour and baking powder, then the fruit and enough milk to give a soft dropping consistency. Turn the mixture into a 2-lb greased and floured loaf tin and bake in the centre of a moderate oven for about 1–1¼ hours.

When the loaf is cold, mix the icing sugar with water so that it is thin enough to pour. Cover the loaf with this and arrange the walnuts and sultanas on top. Eat as a cake when fresh or as a loaf the next day, with butter.

Vanilla Gems   Australia

Makes 12

2 oz melted butter
6 oz self-raising flour
Good pinch of salt
1–2 eggs

8 fl oz milk
1 oz dried fruit (optional)
Few drops vanilla essence

Brush the gem-irons or deep strong patty tins with half the butter. Put into a really hot oven until butter sizzles. Meanwhile, sieve flour and salt, add eggs and beat in milk to make a smooth batter. Add dried fruit if liked, vanilla essence, then remaining butter. Spoon into the very hot gem-irons or patty tins and put back in the oven until the mixture puffs up and is crisp and golden brown. Serve while hot with butter.

Index

Index

216

milk pudding, 94
mince pies, 39
mincemeat, 38
minestrone, 84
Mont Blanc, 78
moules à la marinière, 69
moussaka, 112
mousse, chocolate, 78
muffins, honey, 191
mulligatawny, 161
munkaczina, 104
mushrooms:
  paprika, 55
  on toast, 41
mussels, 69
mustard sauce, 123
mutton:
  kebab with yoghourt, 110
  pilau, 108

nási goreng, 153
Nice, salad from, 73
noodles, 85
  plain fried, 141
Nusstorte, 14

oaties, Scottish, 43
octopus:
  with onions and tomatoes,
    105
  preparing, 105
oliebollen, 27
omelettes:
  Chinese savoury, 146
  crab, 146
  flambé, 77
  rum, 77
  Spanish, 135

orange:
  almond sauce, 179
  baked, 199
  cream, 184
  cream pie, 184
oregano, 83
ossobuco, 91
ovas, pudim de, 136
oxtail soup, 203

pacuszki z kartofli, 51
paella, 134
pancakes:
  cabbage, 54
  cheese, 115
  pineapple, 198
  potato, 51
  Scotch, 43
  stuffed, 52
paprika, 60
Paprikahuhn, 8
paratha, 167
  fillings for, 163
passion fruit:
  cream, 184
  ice cream, 207
pasta, 84
pastry:
  börek, 113
  choux, 79
    fried, 135
pâté choux, 79
peanut cakes, 183
peppers, stuffed, 56
peynirli börek, 114
pies:
  mince, 39
  orange cream, 184

Cookery and Home Management

Sports and Pastimes

These and other PAN Books are obtainable
from all booksellers and newsagents. If you
have any difficulty please send purchase price
plus 5p postage to P.O. Box 11, Falmouth,
Cornwall.